Born into a family of potters in Stoke on Trent, he served in an industrial sandwich course apprenticeship, followed by several years managing a factory. The Suez crisis forced it to close.

He took up medical studies in response to a challenge and to prove his own ability to make his way without his father's help.

Edinburgh Medical School was the world's best in 1957: if he made it there it would be a real triumph.

To the memory of that great sixties' teaching hospital,
Edinburgh Royal Infirmary, in the golden age of the NHS.

John A. T. Duncan

THE BEST OF HEALTH

Tales out of Medical School

AUSTIN MACAULEY PUBLISHERS™

LONDON • CAMBRIDGE • NEW YORK • SHARJAH

A CIP catalogue record for this title is available from the British Library.

ISBN 9781398413276 (Paperback)
ISBN 9781398413283 (ePub e-book)

www.austinmacauley.com

First Published 2021
Austin Macauley Publishers Ltd®
1 Canada Square
Canary Wharf
London
E14 5AA

AND A WARNING!

This is not history, but it contains a moral lesson for those aware of such things. This is an account of a young man struggling through medical training in the mid-twentieth century when things were rather different.

Part One

Suez: A National Disaster and a Personal Crisis

Suez is the point at which this highly personal account starts. My brother, Gregor, and I were industrial potters in our mid-twenties and working as managers in the same factory in Stoke-on-Trent as our father. Some years back, we had served a three-year apprenticeship and now considered ourselves to be fully experienced pottery factory managers. We were eager to strike out for ourselves in an independent family pottery. The Suez crisis changed everything. It was a tsunami that swept through British life, tearing at the wobbly foundations of industry and the armed services alike.

People today, faced with Brexit and its swamp of awful alternatives, can have some idea of what was involved in the Suez crisis in 1956. It was a great wave of successive disasters for British industry, for British society, for Anglo-American unity and for international stability. Suez opened a chasm between the young who had starry ideas about a better world, and the deferential, unthinking older generations who stuck to 'my country, right or wrong'. The debacle ended any belief in the mission of the British to be an exemplary, high-minded and civilised nation, leading the world with assured moral authority.

By its brutally arrogant behaviour in Egypt, the Conservative government set the example for the Soviet Union, a month later, bloodily to suppress the Hungarian bid for independence. Young people in Britain might weep in angry impotence at the scenes of slaughter on the streets of Budapest, but there was nothing that we or our country could do about it.

The invasion of Suez very quickly brought practical punitive consequences for the whole of British industry. OPEC, the mainly Arab association of oil-producing and exporting countries, banned all supplies of oil to Britain. Petrol was suddenly rationed; that was only the start. As at least half of Britain's electricity was produced by oil-fired generators, the Conservative government immediately tried to restrict its industrial use by imposing a 'three-day week'. Power outages became frequent.

Intermittent working proved ruinous in the case of some modern pottery factories, which were heavily committed to continuous electrical furnaces. The older bottle oven factories, such as the one I managed with my brother, were heavily dependent on coal; it too was rationed. As the collieries struggled to keep the electricity generators working, so we struggled to complete our customers' orders before they were cancelled in exasperation. Delivery times for exports just fell off the end of the calendar. Old and modern alike, the pottery factories lost great slices of their export market, in many cases permanently.

Father went off to Australia to look for orders from old clients and new ones. Before leaving, he brought out the whisky bottle to ease a painful conference with his sons. Father was heavily reliant on the old dictum: 'In vino veritas', but decisions floated on alcohol are not at all reliable. On this occasion, his decision was to announce that he was abandoning his long-held ambition to put his accumulated capital into a new pottery factory to be run by his sons. Instead of gambling everything on a fresh venture, he was going to retire at the ripe old age of sixty years and live on his savings.

To end the interview, Father opened the sitting room window and threw the empty whisky bottle into the garden, thus symbolising something or other; bottling out of a bargain with his sons, perhaps. My brother and I drew the same conclusion: we were on our own and need expect no further parental help. We were grown men, and it seemed to us both that it was high time that we leave the nest.

In the bitter winter of 1956/1957, it became obvious that ours was an industry in decline and that many of us must look elsewhere for a new career. Gregor began to make enquiries about emigrating to Australia, or possibly re-enlisting in the Army. I cast my net nearer home, though I, too, began to look at the map of Australia.

Enquiries about apprenticeship schemes with various large companies like Rolls-Royce, The National Coal Board, British Motor Corporation and Unilever produced negative replies. They were interested in graduates but not in untalented dropouts like me. In the shocked and shivering industries after Suez, their dismissive attitude was to be expected. Sadly, many of these companies were about to be put to the sword in a world of commerce that was crueller than anything that had gone before.

To see this required no special intelligence, no foreknowledge of things to come, no magical star. It quickly became apparent to all that because of Suez, the country had dropped over a precipice and was irreparably damaged. Like it or not, a big personal change was forcing itself upon me and many others. It would take both skill and luck to steer this runaway horse of change to a safe stable, and I was no jockey.

'The Vicarage'

I had an old school friend, Tim Showan, an artist of promise, who had just married Betty, a dark-haired beauty from the same Bath School of Art at Chippenham. To be near to their teaching jobs in a market town not far away, they had moved into a couple of rooms in a large old country house, 'The Vicarage', the owner of which had, as they say, 'fallen upon hard times'. I became a frequent visitor.

Stoke-on-Trent was (and probably is still) a place that youngsters abandon at the first opportunity, and I was left behind with very few male friends. An apparently carefree young man with a sports car and a good job, but few friends would probably get so bored that he would marry a local girl; there wasn't much else to do.

With Tim and Betty in their ancient mausoleum of a flat, it was therapeutic to relax in front of a large basket fire in their living room and to build a new world of cigarette smoke. This fire gave both heat and light, two things not always simultaneously present in political discussions on the radio. There were frequent power cuts, so we sat in the flickering illumination of the fire, listening on a battery radio to wise words about the enduring crisis and to stupid justifications of the past. Betty had a rough pregnancy, so the fire often had to be carried on a broad shovel up to their old-fashioned bedroom, also fitted with a large basket fire.

Tim and I would pull up two armchairs beside the glowing fire, while Betty reclined gracefully on her four-poster bed. Thus, the scene was set for profound and searching thoughts about the meaning of things, the price of coal and what the devil John Duncan was going to do with his life.

I was a very unsure young man and struggled with a feeling of inferiority, possibly because everything so far had been made smooth for me. It is easy to succeed in the industry if your father is a senior director of the business. Vanity had not blinded me to the fact that I had been promoted over men, only a few years older, who had recently been on active service in the armed forces. Furthermore, I had been excused from national service on the flimsy grounds of 'hay fever' and, fresh out of school, had easily passed all the industrial examinations required for the management of a pottery factory.

They, on the other hand, had wasted years in the armed forces and had then to struggle for yet more years doing night classes to get their technical qualifications. We had nothing in common. These rather older men hated my guts and rightly so. While they had spent the years of their youth in the armed services, their reward was to be pushed aside by twerps like me. This was why it was important to succeed in something difficult and to stand upon my own achievements.

Applications to Medical Schools

As so often happens, the answer came quite casually and from an unexpected direction. The current girlfriend of the winter months was the daughter of a GP. One Saturday night while I waited for her to apply the finishing touches to her war

15

paint, I sat for a while with the worthy doctor, who was reading the *British Medical Journal*. His daughter had obviously briefed him about my casting around for another career, so he didn't now view me as marriage material.

Jokingly, he pointed to the article he had just read in the *BMJ*: "The Dean of Medicine in Edinburgh is suggesting here that his medical school should recruit more students from non-scientific backgrounds. Why don't you apply?"

So I did.

Just about the middle of November, I wrote applications to fifteen medical schools in England and Scotland, explaining my position as a mature student with a technical but not scientific background. Eight replied, calling me to interview, but from Edinburgh, there came only silence.

I attended wintery interviews in London, Sheffield, Manchester and Liverpool, excusing myself from the factory with a story of repeated injuries from weekend club rugby. My brother, Gregor, took over the management of the factory on these various days through January, February and March. Nobody seemed bothered by this.

Gregor enjoyed being in full charge and made a few significant alterations. We agreed that our long-term future lay wrapped in woolly uncertainty but definitely not in the Potteries. Gregor looked at Australia, while I looked at British medical schools.

A Series of Winter Interviews at Various Medical Schools

New Year's Day wasn't much celebrated in post-war England; in fact, the Stoke-on-Trent City Police New Year

16

ball of 1955/1956 ended at 11:30 pm because the town hall keeper insisted on locking the building before midnight. London, too, for all its fooling around in Trafalgar Square at midnight, treated 1 January as just another working day. For this reason and its own inclination, Middlesex Hospital called me for an interview at 2:00 pm that day.

Indian food was unknown to the Potteries in 1956/1957, but there in Gower Street, just yards away from the Middlesex, was an obliging Punjabi restaurant. I had absolutely no idea what the menu meant (I thought that chapatis were probably Indian chips). This place was handy, and I felt hungry.

With my breath laden with curry and my stomach rumbling rather rudely, I was ushered into the Dean's presence. In a rather narrow, gloomy office on the ground floor of this imposing neo-Georgian building was a small man in a city suit. His hair was black and shiny, and his horn-rimmed glasses were circles of disdain. He sat writing at a roll-top desk in an office just wide enough to fit a standard casement window for ventilation purposes. As the light from this window was inadequate for reading, the Dean had a table lamp perched on top of his desk.

"Duncan?" he asked, before returning to his writing.

A long pause lengthened into a minute, a minute and a half, and two minutes of silence.

"This is bloody ridiculous," I thought as the stomach rumbles forced out a silent fart. It was becoming imperative to make this interview short.

This Dean was playing games with me. It had happened before. Important men like to impress and use silence to crumble the self-confidence of the interviewee. The best defence is to conduct the interview yourself. It should always be easier to answer your own questions, especially if you have had four hours on a slow train to prepare yourself for the obvious, such as:

'Why do you wish to change course at your age?'

'Why do you wish to study medicine?'

'Why Middlesex Hospital?'

And it goes on.

I ran through the lot in five minutes and felt that I might be cutting things a bit fine; the fire in my belly had nothing to do with my ardour for Middlesex Hospital. I stopped speaking.

The Dean said without looking up, "We'll let you know."

He went on writing in his dark, cramped office. My thoughts had already turned elsewhere. The head porter directed me to a door many yards down a gloomy corridor. In the cold winter dark of the men's toilet, the embarrassing curry left me. I didn't expect to hear from that disagreeable Dean again (though, strangely, he accepted me).

The train home was waiting for me at Euston. I tipped my hat over my eyes because, in those days, serious men wore a trilby, and I was a serious man. Weary exhaustion wrapped me in sleep. Wherever I studied medicine, it would not be in London.

The Sheffield interview was in March, by which time petrol rationing had become a worn joke, so without qualm, I drove over the wintry Derbyshire and Yorkshire hills. In my very comfortable, heavy, shiny Triumph sports car, I slipped and slithered over the city's tramlines and fumbled through the centre to find the medical school. In a pleasant interview, it may have done me some good to mention that I thought highly of the Sheffield Medical School because its professor of biochemistry had just been awarded a Nobel Prize. They offered me a place.

An interview in Liverpool the following week was also very pleasant, though somehow it became a discussion of Russian literature and the relative merits of Tolstoy versus Dostoevsky. The university area was difficult to approach from the South. My main memory is of the Mersey Tunnel, and how driving down its steep slope induced in me feelings of vertigo, reminding me of Alice's falling and falling and falling into Wonderland. They, too, offered me a place.

Manchester was not a success. The day was wintery and road conditions bad, so I took the train, arriving forty minutes later than scheduled time. There was no time for lunch, even if I could have found a likely place, so I arrived at the Dean's office with five minutes to spare and a hollow stomach rumbling but this time in a plaintive way, rather than a menacing fashion. The interview went badly; it was entirely my fault.

The letter calling me to interview had fixed the time for 2:00 pm, but I was kept waiting until 2:45 pm on a wooden bench in a long, draughty corridor lined with bilious green encaustic tiles. The place had all the appeal of a Victorian public lavatory and smelled similarly of cheap disinfectant. The interviewers, two anonymous grey men, were similarly unappealing. One, a long, thin presence, stayed silent throughout my fifteen minutes; the other shorter and plumper, adopted the languid pose of one who really doesn't enjoy this sort of thing.

I shot a line about being impressed with the scientific advances made in medicine and made the mistake of mentioning Sheffield and the Nobel Prize. That was a daft thing to do when I had absolutely no idea what Krebs Cycle was, nor how many wheels it had.

"You know," said the languid one. "We have better things to do than pander to discontented young men. Have you never thought that in your work as a potter, you might one day make the perfect piece?"

What a fatuous thing to say! How terribly Edwardian! Straight out of Oscar Wilde. How quaint!

What did he know about working in a dirty old factory; doing the same repetitive task all day and tracing a lifetime through fifty wasted years? He enraged me. I groped for an absolutely devastating reply but only succeeded in: "I'm afraid the industrial ethos is rather more demanding than to allow a lifetime. My factory must produce five thousand perfect pots per day or two million per year. Even the great Wedgwood, when he produced his copy of the Portland Vase, made twenty to take account of faults, and wastage and gifts to valued clients."

I had blown it at Manchester, and I knew it was my own fault that they did not offer me a place. There followed a long chilly April; while my brother and I continued to run the factory, we tried to smarten up the running of the place and even started to make our own oval saggars, by which means we reckoned to save one hundred pounds per week.

Gregor found a saggar maker and a saggar maker's bottom knocker and had a den made for them right by the bottle ovens. You probably don't know what I'm writing about but don't worry, I thought that a dab of local colour would brighten the narrative. At last, Edinburgh Medical School is about to appear like a swallow in the summer.

Acceptance

One Saturday morning, the post came clattering through the large letterbox of No. 2 Milehouse Lane at 7 o'clock. A stiff white envelope bore the news that Edinburgh University, without even clapping eyes on me, was offering me a place in its medical school and rather imperiously demanded a reply within five days. With eager excitement, a letter of acceptance was written, followed by a brisk walk down to the GPO in Newcastle-u-Lyme, just to be sure that it caught the midday post to Edinburgh. My fate was decided in the manner of a Victorian novel, where a letter from abroad provides the solution to a difficult problem.

Edinburgh in 1957

Edinburgh is unique among the cities of the world in the honour that it bestows upon the medical profession. A statue to immortalise (or at least to remind us for a while of), a doctor stands at either end of its main thoroughfare, Princes Street. At the East End, the explorer, Dr David Livingstone awaits the arrival of Stanley, hard by Waverley Station, while Sir James Y. Simpson, pioneer of painless childbirth with chloroform, sits expectantly waiting at the West End, near the old Caledonian Railway Station, now called The Waldorf Hotel.

Queen Victoria's statue still sits on top of the National Gallery, supervising the flow of traffic up and down Princes Street. No longer the dazzling boulevard that delighted our Edwardian ancestors, nevertheless, Princes Street's open Southern vista of the castle on a craggy rock with flower gardens at its feet still attracts photographers from all over the world. That combination of the savage rocks and a formal garden lessens the impact of the street's north side now, alas, bereft of its unique blend of restaurants, tea shops, coffee shops, chocolate houses, fruiters, tobacconists and splendid emporia. A facade of cheapjack shops on a row of concrete boxes has long since replaced Victorian comeliness with the lifeless and makeshift architecture of the fast-buck trader.

Despite all this, Edinburgh was and remains a city whose beauty dazzled a young man from the Potteries. There was simply no way to compare the great Athens of the North with the dirtiest urban area in Europe. The Potteries was not so much a city as an administrative label of convenience to describe the urban sprawl of seven large industrial villages strung along the valley of the River Trent. Somehow or other, the casino of life sent me North to wander the broad streets and parklands of the most beautiful city in Europe.

The bold decision in the early nineteenth century to drain the swampy wasteland between the new Georgian buildings of Princes Street and the ragged rocks of the castle enabled the construction, a little later, of the main railway line right through the centre of the city and the cultivation of the rest as a decorative garden. The physical separation of old Edinburgh from the New Town serves to emphasise its many faces. This is the town of Jekyll & Hyde, of John Knox and the Enlightenment, of the burgeoning anatomical teaching centre and Burke & Hare.

A city so experienced at concealing the amazing, even disturbing, beneath a tranquil surface of seeming smug satisfaction is a city capable of the most extreme surprises. In 1957, its citizens might give the impression of being content to live a decade in the past, but their carefully planned New Town was nearly two hundred years in advance of the times.

During the Enlightenment of the eighteenth century, through the nineteenth century and the birth of 'scientific medicine', and right into the twentieth century with the new age of powerful drugs, there has been a special affinity between Edinburgh and medicine, as it were, between town and operating gown. In 1956, it was, in Edinburgh, commonly agreed that this was the finest medical school in the world and that, therefore, Edinburgh Royal Infirmary was the finest teaching hospital in the world. This intense loyalty had been expressed for two hundred and fifty years through the pennies of the poor and the pounds of the rich.

The endowment fund of the Royal Infirmary reached into the millions even before 1948, and large gifts were recorded on boards lining the main corridor, on bronze plaques (one point two five million pounds from the Scottish Miners' Union) and with the occasional marble bust. The walls bore lists of donations dating back to 1700, some small (ten pounds), some millions but most gathered in mites. This cash was backed up by the endowment of many acres of land around the city. Where this considerable charitable endowment fund is now, after the hospital PFI scheme removed it to Petty France, is not known to me.

The medical profession returned the town's enthusiasm by competing strenuously for the honour of being on the teaching staff of the Royal Infirmary, even though the appointment meant that they must abandon their private practice. To be 'on' at the Royal was to have reached the ultimate height of success in a medical career. This applied equally to a nurse becoming a ward sister at ERI: there was no higher to go.

With the River Forth two miles to the North, the old Royal Infirmary of Edinburgh was screened from Princes Street by the grim fortifications of the castle and the tall tenements of the Royal Mile. About fifteen minutes brisk walk in a southerly direction from the centre of the great street, up the Mound, across the sinuous, cobbled spine of the Old Town, over the eleven (or twelve) hidden spans of George IV Bridge and past the statue of Greyfriars Bobby, brought those in need of medical help or learning to the gates of the great teaching hospital.

Edinburgh Royal Infirmary spread itself in Scottish Baronial Gothic splendour over eleven acres of the grassy meadows, where until the mid-nineteenth century, cows were grazed. The splendid stone confection of pointed spires and turrets now serves a different purpose, but the coat of arms over its main portal still depicts the mythical pelican, tearing its own breast to feed its young. It is a poignant reminder that until it entered the National Health Service in 1948, Edinburgh Royal Infirmary was the largest charity hospital in Europe.

At the stroke of a ministerial pen, the NHS gained an enormous centre of medical excellence, a world-famous medical school and a staff of doctors and nurses who were proud to belong to it. As one learned law lord put it: "Nursing in the ERI is a better finishing school for my daughter than any in Switzerland."

The city that awaited me when I arrived at the Caledonian Station one dark October evening in 1957 was shrouded in misty gloom but prickling with pinpoints of moving light.

Thus, with a fleeting glimpse, began my long love affair with a beautiful city, wrapped in the mystery of hidden secrets. This station, now long gone, formed a curious arrowhead terminus within the A-shaped building of the posh Caledonian Hotel. Platforms, taxi rank, refreshment rooms, everything was under cover of the vaulted glass roof supported on the two arms of the A.

The train was two hours later than advertised. It was dark and drizzling; my new address lay somewhere out there. Luckily, in the A-shaped covered courtyard of the station, several young men were taking taxis. People in Stoke-on-Trent took a taxi only in the direst emergency; otherwise, such things were regarded as an unjustifiable luxury, typical of a soft life in London. This situation was an emergency that demanded that thrift be thrown to the wind. There wasn't a snowball's chance of managing my luggage on a bus (even if I had known which one to take). I joined the queue.

As these very vocal young men sorted themselves into groups to share a taxi, I recognised one or two faces from the train. Two youths in front of me in the line were going to the same University Hall of Residence, so we shared the ride. The taxi from Caledonian Station drove through a dark and drizzly city to the Dalkeith Road and dropped the three of us, together with a pile of luggage, outside a dimly lit Scottish baronial stone mansion, standing in its own grounds. Unbidden, a welcome party appeared to help us carry our baggage inside the spikily turreted house of Salisbury Green.

Salisbury Green

Battleship linoleum in monotonous light brown covered every square inch of every floor, and all lights were of the lowest wattage in the interest of economy. This was the Salisbury Green University Hall of Residence for Men, and its chatelaine was advancing upon me as I stood, suddenly alone, in the hallway. The two second-year vets, who had shared the taxi with me were obviously former residents of Salisbury Green returning for a second helping, but to avoid conversation with the matron in grey, they had disappeared to their former rooms with their buddies. I was a new boy who still had to be formally enrolled in this creaky stillness that smelled of furniture polish and boiled cabbage.

In the office on the first floor sat a large matronly woman in her late fifties whose rather aggressive demeanour concealed an even more warlike nature. Her grey hair was scraped back into a severe bun, forming a curve symmetrical with her sharply jutting chin and her eagle's beak of a nose, thus giving her the profile of a well-sharpened battle-axe. She glared across her desk as she took my details from the university's formal letter allocating me to her care.

"There will be no drink in this house, and no women except on Sunday afternoon when they can take tea in the front sitting room or in the music room."

This was said in emphatic tones that brooked no contradiction.

"The front door will be locked at 10:00 pm, but you may apply to me for a key if you expect to be out later. That key must be deposited in the special box on my office door. No student may have his own key."

26

"Breakfast is from 8:00 am to 9:00 am. The evening meal is from 6:00 pm to 7:00 pm. All bedrooms must be vacated by 9:30 am to allow the cleaners to do their work. You will make your own bed, and you will make your own arrangements for laundry.

"You are expected to behave at all times quietly, in a gentlemanly way and to remember that your fellow residents are here, like you, to study.

"My office is open to you between 9:00 am and 8:00 pm. Please bear in mind that I have a free hand from the Director of Student Welfare to deal severely with bad behaviour."

I balanced my serious man's hat on my knee and looked around the room to see if there were indeed a cat-o'-nine-tails or possibly an Irish shillelagh hanging on the wall. This was all a bit like a boys' reformatory school.

This grey, somewhat overweight dragon had the assistance of a residents committee in ruling the house of forty-five young men with a live-in kitchen staff of three young women and daily cleaning staff of eight. She provided me with a quick tour of this rambling old house and an enduring introduction to upper-class Morningside Edinburgh English. In a previous life, she might have worked with Muriel Spark's fictitious Miss Jean Brodie, the ultra-genteel teacher.

Getting to her feet and tightening the leather belt, from which dangled a large bunch of keys, she led me to the rear of this shambling mansion by way of short corridors and twisty passages until we reached a large double room, elevated above the linoleum corridor by four steps. Inside the darkroom, there could be seen the pale square of a skylight, while through a lower-level dormer window loomed the massive dark shadow of the biggest bloody spoil tip that I had ever seen. The Potteries' skyline was ragged with pyramids of coal bings and spoil tips, but I had seen nothing as big as this.

In the morning, I was greeted by the green glory of Arthur's Seat shining through the window.

My intended roommate was expected to be a few days late, as he was travelling from Trinidad by sea. He was not a Caribbean Islands scholar, of whom there were many; he was coming by oil tanker because his father was a medical officer to an oil company. Nor was this an accidental pairing, for he, too, had a non-science background. He too was one of the Dean of Medicine's 'guinea pigs'.

Together we set about testing the assertion that medical students could be selected simply from the brightest of any discipline. In the case of my roommate, Nial Findlayson, he was completely vindicated. Nial rose to the very top of the medical profession. Other students chosen in this intake included a decorated Battle of Britain fighter pilot and one or two middle-aged women, desperately seeking a new start. They all justified the Dean's confidence.

This large cool room with its tight little window onto parkland was, accordingly, all mine for a little while. These days, Salisbury Green is an upmarket hotel run by the university and its ample park is covered with the more modern style of halls of residence for both male and female students. The whole campus bears the name of Sir Donald Pollock, the shipping magnate who gifted not only this site, but large areas of central Edinburgh property to the university at the time when Sir Edward Appleton was Principal.

Appleton was a Nobel Laureate whose work on the ionosphere enabled the creation of radar just before World War II, and he lived in a large stone mansion, just over the garden wall from Salisbury Green. He was a jolly old soul and would amiably return cricket balls smacked for six off our large lawns by our talented West Indian residents.

Looking around my new room, which was to be my home for a year, I discovered that my trunk had arrived in my room before me. It was unmistakably mine because it was a large plywood box with two very large hinged handles. I had bought it from one of the many ex-WD stores that were selling off army surplus equipment, principally clothing but also including these chests, which had been intended to contain medical supplies. It was just right, being both robust and cheap.

For reasons that remain obscure, in 1957, the War Department was disposing of a large amount of orange-coloured paint. I bought a pot and gave the new trunk a couple of coats both inside and out. Then I wrote in large capitals: JOHN A. T. DUNCAN. There was no mistaking the ownership of this box.

It was nearly 10 o'clock, and I had had a long day: eight hours on the train, with no meal waiting for me. That didn't matter: I'd arrived. The students that I met on the express from Crewe all had moved off to the restaurant car at 4:00 pm for a hearty afternoon tea. They were wise to the way that landladies tended to lock their dining room against late arrivals.

In those days, trains into the Caledonian station were nearly always late. As British Rail teas were enjoyable and affordable, it was an obvious precaution for students to fill up before arriving in Edinburgh to face some snorting dragon of a landlady.

Having disposed of the leather belted chatelaine, I looked at the bed. It was a strange bed, an old extending army cot, a narrow U-shaped trough, whose good point was its adjustable length. Everything was clean, and I slept like a hunting dog.

The breakfast, next morning, was ample and good: fried fish, little dabs cooked in butter, six of them with the option of seconds. The atmosphere was a little strained due to the presence of many former private schoolboys who seemed to have an aversion to conversation mixed with food. It was, therefore, a surprise that one such large example seated near me around a table with twenty others announced in a loud voice: "Poo! Somebody is wearing perfume."

He was rather obviously referring to my aftershave. It was rather strong; quite revolting, in fact, but this matter had to be tackled head-on. Things might get bloody. It required a full-frontal assault, but it had to be toned down by recycling a bit of dialogue from a recent movie to prevent it from appearing too brutal.

"When you are old enough to need a razor, you too will find aftershave stops the skin from smarting afterwards."

We both stood back from the table. He wanted to hit me but then thought the better of it. That was a wise decision for both of us. A fight would have wasted time when we both needed urgently to get to the 9 o'clock lecture. His aggressive attitude to a complete stranger, nevertheless, puzzled me. It became all the more necessary to sort out his problem when it became apparent later in the day that he and a fellow second-year vet occupied the room next to mine in Salisbury Green.

After supper that evening, I grabbed this guy's arm as he left the room and steered him into the deserted billiards room.

"Come on, let's get sorted. Why were you looking for a fight this morning?"

Then it all came out. There was a girl involved, but the whole thing was nonsense based on recycled hearsay. Peace was declared.

A few nights later, the vet students sealed the armistice with a few pints of beer at 'The Sheep Heid' in nearby Duddingston village. The whole resident body of shiny-faced and confident young men walked out there for an evening of beer and skittles. Their return order might have reminded Napoleon of his retreating army returning from Moscow: some limping, some staggering but most in good order.

Beer & Skittles at Duddingston

The skittle alley is still there, and an evening of old fashioned beer and skittles is still a great way to unwind and make new friends. Old-style alleys are nothing like the modern, highly mechanised commercial equivalent. We had to hire the alley from the landlord of the 'Sheep Heid', and he furnished us with two young men to set up the nine-pin diamond ('they'll take halves of beer, ye ken') to keep the score and to bring in the mutton pies at half time.

The heavy round balls were difficult to manage until we discovered the thumb hole, which helped us get a grip. There were smaller balls for ladies, which, of course, we all avoided, being beer-drinking grown men. The big balls were, nevertheless, a problem to use because, whereas the

American-style bowling alleys provide twenty feet or so of launch pad, the 'Sheep Heid' allowed just three cramped feet.

Some solved the problem of obtaining maximum muzzle velocity by holding the big ball in two hands and hurling themselves forward to land flat on the floor but with their feet still behind the white line. Others just rolled the ball and let the slope do its work.

The alley of polished timber rumbled just as loudly as it had when Bonnie Prince Charlie's men had used the old inn, near his headquarters in 1745 and rumble it certainly did. The clatter and crash of falling skittles acted as a counterpoint to the slow 'clonk' of the returning balls forming an orderly line in the ball trough and the boom of the big ball rolling for the twenty-five feet length of the alley. A slight downhill inclination deceived the novice by hiding, as it did, an unequal camber, sloping both left and right; it increased the ball's velocity but did nothing to help it find the centre pin. Accuracy and skill were noticeably absent from our game.

We settled our account and, full of beer and bonhomie, staggered home from Duddingston along the road that skirts Arthur's Seat, with the ruddy rocks of Abraham's Ribs on our right, past the Wells O' Weary on our left. Many years ago, the Wells had been a place of public execution and was supposedly haunted by the ghosts of those hanged there. We shambled raggedly back to Salisbury Green, in decidedly non-regimental order but good humour, nevertheless. Some of the younger members of the company felt a little dizzy, no doubt.

This was understandable: they were very young, and this was their first encounter with more than two pints of beer. As we passed through the great wild garden that surrounded both the men's hall and the ladies' hall, St Leonards, we gave a chorus of 'Goodnight, Ladies'. Very droll, very witty; very daring.

For some reason, nobody had thought to ask for a door key, but the wiser older residents simply put a finger to their lip and tiptoed around the building to look into the large music room. We learned then that the huge sash window was faulty and could always be slid open, so in we all went.

Freshers' Week

Freshers' Week that strangely subdued teenage ritual started with a formal reception given by the University Senate in the Upper Library of the main university building. This grandly imposing Georgian piece was designed by an Edinburgh architect named Playfair and this Upper Library was a long barrel-vaulted tunnel of pillars and embossed ceilings, splendid in scarlet, cream and gold. The various deans of faculty were assembled in the middle of the room with the Principal.

The long line of incoming freshers shook hands with a Nobel Laureate, for many the only time in their life that they would clasp the hand of fame. Their other hand clasped a glass of white wine with which to drink whatever toast followed Principal Appleton's address.

The young undergraduates were fresh and friendly in their enthusiasm, but they all had an urgent desire to talk about themselves, which I found annoying when I wanted to talk about myself. My absolute ignorance of Scottish private schools betrayed a very middle England assumption that the whole of Britain was much like Manchester or Birmingham or Tyneside. Private education, we believed, had been rendered obsolete by the Butler Act of 1944. Provincial scorn for further education was encapsulated in G. B. Shaw's dictum: "Those who can, do; the others teach."

Nobody at Wolstanton Grammar School had mentioned in 1950 that there were any universities in Scotland. As for the many private/public secondary schools, it was all too easy for an Englishman to give offence. In England, a school generally bore the name of the city or town where it stood. It was confusing to be confronted in Edinburgh with personal names, such as 'George Heriot's School, 'George Watson's' and so on.

Far better to nod and mutter 'Ah, yes' than to offend the locals. To be frank, having arrived at the Upper Library of Edinburgh University, was it not time to let go of the comfort blanket of private secondary education?

A remorseless stream of arrivals created a current of people moving straight down the central aisle of the library, pausing briefly with the Principal and then dividing right and left into two contraflows, puddling into the many alcoves of the library. Carefully circulating through and around knots and clumps of youngsters who obviously shared an Edinburgh background I looked carefully at the female students scattered around the crowded long, narrow room.

A group of American girls immediately came into focus, mainly because they looked more mature than their UK contemporaries but also because they were well dressed and were failing to mix in a way that left them solitary as a rock in the surging tide of people. Stranded in an alcove of the library, they talked about themselves. This they were very happy to do and soon supplied me with a league table of US universities.

Strangely enough, they were all at the end of their second year in one of the top ten 'schools', as they called them, and were all reading Arts subjects of the type that I had myself rejected at an earlier age. All, without prompting by me, but probably responding reflexively to some US convention, volunteered an outline of their parents' social standing, business seniority, and house size. In 1957, a six-bedroom house with seven bathrooms seemed absurd, but maybe there was a possibility that they may also have meant 'WC' when they spoke of 'bathroom'.

Dunlop's Lecture of Welcome

The introductory lecture to medical freshers was given in the anatomy lecture theatre by Dr Dunlop, an eminent physician, who became Regis Professor of Medicine the next year and a knight the year after that. His lean patrician profile strongly resembled that of the Iron Duke of Wellington whose effigy, opposite the GPO on Princes Street, by a sculptor named Steele was cast in bronze. He was the very model of a distinguished physician, silver-haired, tall and handsome. Most doctors think that they are good teachers, but very few are great teachers.

Dunlop was a great teacher, whose lectures so gripped the attention of his audience that they took no notes but listened carefully instead. Many specialists, learned and wise, write textbooks of mind-bending dullness; not he. His books could be read as a form of relaxation after a long day.

The anatomy lecture theatre was a relic of Burke & Hare. Ever-widening concentric arcs of channel iron rose in ten tiers in front of steeply raked wooden benches, forming a funnel focused on the lecturer's table. The flat side of the channel iron yielded a shelf six inches wide for a notebook or for elbows but was too hard and cold for the weary head of a deadbeat student. In the days when medical education was heavily reliant on knowledge of anatomical structures, an operation would be performed in this central space of the lecture theatre, with spectators craning and peering from a distance to follow the process.

This belief in distance learning held sway even into the 1930s when several operating theatres in the old Royal Infirmary were rebuilt and included a viewing gallery. The sad truth is that at this range, very little can be seen. One might as well try to instruct a midshipman in the rigging of a sailing ship by giving him a telescope and a seat on the deck.

Reported speech can only hope to give the flavour, however faint, of the opening address to the new medical students. Sixty years on, I still regard this man as representing all that was best in Edinburgh's golden age of medicine.

"I hope that there are none of those pitiful people with notebooks present here. My medical lectures are already much better written in your textbooks. Today, I want you to listen to me.

"I welcome you to the greatest school of medicine in the world to begin your medical studies in the finest profession in the world. During the winter and spring, I read many application forms written by idealistic young people eager to make the world a better place. Hold tight to your ideals and cherish them through the long years of study and work ahead.

"Medicine is a wonderful garden of fruit and flowers. There are so many diverse paths to follow that almost every personal interest can find fulfilment. You are privileged to be given the freedom of this beautiful garden.

"Yours is the largest first-year intake ever, with the largest proportion of young women ever. As a matter of policy, the Medical Faculty will henceforth reserve thirty per cent of its annual intake of students to females. I warn you now that the first three years will prove too much for about twenty per cent of you, so your numbers will drop from two hundred and forty to less than two hundred. I must also warn you here and now that only about five per cent of you will be able to find jobs in Edinburgh after graduation.

"These will mostly be those timid creatures who have never ventured beyond the city boundaries and whose well-established parents or uncles are saving a seat for them in the family practice. Such people don't know what magic the great world holds for a graduate of the Edinburgh Medical School. Your MBChB degree will be a passport to travel the world. You will be welcomed throughout the English-speaking world.

"For those of you who choose to remain in the UK, there are people all over this island who regard an Edinburgh doctor with such high esteem that they will seek him or her however far they have to travel.

"I deeply envy you the opportunity to work from the start of your career in this NHS, which allows you to treat your patients according to their needs and not, as has been the case in the past, according to their means. When I stood at the threshold of medicine in 1920, there were at my disposal less than twenty drugs that are still in use or recognised to be of therapeutic value. But you, like gods upon Mount Olympus, you will hurl your Jovian therapeutic thunderbolts at disease and illness. You will never be rich in the NHS, but you will not have to make a living by being the poodle of the rich valetudinarians of Edinburgh and London."

The Class Photograph (and St Trinians)

Full of optimism, we trooped out into the Medical Quad to find ourselves confronted by a large semi-circle of tables at which a tall man in a dark suit was pointing large mahogany and brass camera mounted on a brass cog and tooth mechanism. Men and women, we were marshalled into place by servitors and others, for he was Edinburgh's foremost photographer. Seats in the middle front were reserved for a dozen professorial staff, with the Dean in the centre.

The staff were flanked by good-looking female students showing off their comely legs, while the men were arranged by height: shorties behind the chairs, bigger ones behind, then the rest in a nice symmetrical arrangement on the tables. Then came the big surprise. Large cards were handed out bearing numbers.

It was time for mug shots!

These would be attached to our as yet slender record file so that in future examinations, our identity could be checked to prevent impersonation, a wicked US practice that had been used in Ivy League universities by the sons of the super-rich.

This distribution was followed by a delay, while we awaited the arrival of the Dean and Faculty. Economically and frugally, old group photographs had been cut up to use for these numbered cards, so there was a picture on the reverse side. I looked hard at mine and found that I had the central section of a girls school called St Trinians taken in 1937, naming the headmistress as 'Miss Searle'. In those days, nearly everyone knew about the fictional girls of St Trinians, illustrated by Ronald Searle.

He must have founded the Gothic horror of St Trinians on the school that his aunt ran in Edinburgh, and here was the photographic proof. The weird building now called St Leonards Hall of residence for ladies was the real thing, complete with water spouts as stone cannons poking out of the spiky turrets. And it stood in the same grounds, only yards away from our own Salisbury Green hall of residence.

This rare find was quickly removed by a squad of servitors at the exit from the Quad who took the numbered card and recorded the name of the person who had held it for the group photograph. There were no more lectures that day so that medical freshers could pass through the bureaucracy of registering at Adam House, where admission cards and matriculation cards were duly issued. Those of us hoping to receive grants were given notice of our fees, even though we were not paying customers. We then had to troop back to the Dean of Medicine's office in the Medical Quad to sign a second matriculation document.

This office stood at the head of a long ceremonial covered stairway and declined to open its door before 12 noon. A thick queue of medical students stood impatiently waiting for fifteen minutes. From the young men standing around me on the stair, I formed several good friendships. Our meetings, sadly, are now very occasional, being limited to a drink on class anniversaries. As we are now past our fiftieth, perhaps there will not be many at our sixtieth.

Freshers' Fair & Reception

After lunch in the Men's Union with another act of membership and fee of one pound, a group of us wandered back to the Old College to taste the Freshers Fair. All sorts and varieties of clubs and organisations competed for our interest. I joined the British Medical Students' Association (BMSA) because it was free and had a most colourful scarf; the Athletic Club fancying a game or two of Rugby and possibly some cross-country running to keep me fit; the University Gymnasium also because it was free to use upon production of a matriculation card. Being a serious young man, an invitation was also accepted to take coffee with the Anglican Students' pastor near the Chalmers Hospital.

It crossed my mind that having had quite enough of the Young Conservatives in the Potteries and being totally opposed to the Conservatives in Westminster, the Student Labour Party club might offer some intelligent conversation.

Long hair and long wind seem often to go together in politics, and sure enough, I was soon cornered by a young male student of such a description. With little or no introduction, he commenced a loud vocal examination of my knowledge of Marx and Lenin. As he showed no interest in my counter questions on Attlee and Bevan, I concluded that he was showing off in order to impress a large young lady in an equally large scarlet sweater.

I don't know about the young lady, but I was not impressed then with student politics and never have been since. Students, by very definition, lack the experience of life that comes with the years. They reach for off-the-bookshelf solutions. This belief that they are pioneers of original thoughts makes them appear rather condescending.

They do not seem to realise that these remedies to social ills are like bits of plumbing pipe and have to fit one into the other; they are not necessarily mutually compatible. In real life, the communities at the receiving end may have their own quite different ideas and needs.

The evening brought The Freshers Ball in the McEwan Hall, an imposing rotunda, mostly used for graduations. Mythological deities painted on walls and ceiling reclined in flowing robes of pre-Raphaelite brilliance, their colours making the borrowed or cut-down dresses of eighteen-year-old schoolgirls look rather drab. This imposing drum of space rose into three gilded balconies and could contain about two thousand people at graduation times. For workaday things such as the weekly organ recitals at lunchtime, only the ground floor was used, being liberally provided with rows of chairs. The American girls did not attend, so I lost interest and went home.

An Encounter with Venus

It occurred to me that being an arts student, the American girl may well be found around noon in the Common Room of the Old College. Sure enough, she was there with her handmaidens surrounding her. By daylight, she seemed smaller without high heels and her features less well defined without make up, but the overall impression was still very appealing. A date was arranged without difficulty; indeed, I was to pick her up from her digs in Ramsey Gardens the following evening.

I had been in Edinburgh only a few days, so the address meant nothing to me. The postman who dropped the morning mail onto the glass-topped outer table at Salisbury Green gave me brief directions, warning me that there was 'a hell of a lot of stairs in the Ramsay Gardens tenements'.

People in the Potteries did not live in tenements, so Ramsey Gardens seemed a bit dodgy in prospect. In the gloom of a wet October evening, I walked apprehensively up the Royal Mile toward the Castle esplanade. Ramsey Gardens was tucked away in the corner of the castle esplanade, or parade ground in common parlance. The sharp approach up slippery cobbles with sudden steep winding stairs leading to nail-studded doors looked like the entry to a robbers' lair.

A massive iron ring served as a door knocker. My summons was answered by a very pleasant middle-aged lady who led me into an elegant sitting room, the windows of which displayed a wonderful view of a lamp-lit Princes Street animated by the lights of the traffic moving slowly along it. In those days, none of the shops along Princes Street had anything so vulgar as a neon sign advertising its name; instead, they illuminated their window display but only up to 10:00 pm. This Edinburgh matron with her upper-class intonation reminded me of the way the wife of a company chairman or managing director would behave at the works dinner dances that had been compulsory attendance in the Potteries.

A few words of light conversation reminded me also that I was being surveyed for suitability and made me glad that I had worn my serious man's hat. It also became apparent that she was indeed the wife of a bank director. Miss USA was there temporarily, as a favour to her father, another seriously elevated banker. The good lady had taken it upon herself to book a table for us at a nightclub that combined food and dancing, so that was all sorted. All I had to do was be a charming partner. It really was a works dance in miniature!

By the time Miss Honey appeared, I had been examined on my knowledge of Highland life, of which I knew nothing, my familiarity with private school education, which was nil, and my prospects in general, which were unclear at their very best. The girl, nevertheless, looked worth the quizzing that the wait had entailed.

The waiter in this first-floor place of expensive entertainment, which, for embellishment, I'll call 'Buffies', produced two menus with a flourish.

"I can recommend the grouse. It's very well hung, and there's a very good claret to go with it if sir would like to order it."

Cheeky bugger! But then Miss America thought this was a good suggestion, so we had it, and politely spat little pellets of lead into the ashtray provided.

The atmosphere was good; the lights subdued and the string trio provided romantic background music. As we danced on the tiny space provided, the waiter circled around with our second bottle of claret.

She looked at me across the rim of her wine glass. The candle's steady light made her blue eyes shade to green, but they seemed to focus on some distant object. Slowly but unmistakably, Miss Honeybun was getting drunk. I had to get her back to Ramsey Gardens before she passed out or Madame the Chairman's wife would play hell, and she was the sort who would take her anger right to the topmost authority; might even get me sent down. I settled a wine inflated bill and left no tip; I obviously still needed enough for a taxi.

That should have been that, but within three weeks, I needed a partner for the Salisbury Green November ball. Miss USA had moved to a flat above the shops on Princes Street, but I had her phone number from Madam Chairman. This time an Edinburgh Corporation bus provided our transport to the dance.

The entertainments and decorations were organised by a group of young men, and they had not forgotten to provide a cash bar. How different, how much more beautiful the young student women seemed when they were scrubbed up, yet how boyish their young partners seemed. Surely, these were not the same young people that I had looked at so dismissively at the Freshers' Ball? This was a quite different selection.

The band was a student sextet with a very gifted pianist who led the group through Strauss waltzes, Victor Sylvester selections and on to Rock and Roll. It was a great dance, lubricated by frequent visits to the bar and therein lay the fly floating on the whisky. Miss America shifted half a bottle of Scotch; I moved the other half. Damned if I was going to drink lemonade while she guzzled the hard stuff!

There was a pop song in 1952 about a young man who spent his all on a girl. Its words came back to me as we left Salisbury Green's party: "She was peaches; she was honey and she cost me all my money."

It was about a mile from the Dalkeith Road to Princes Street, and buses were few at 12:00 on a Saturday night. My girlfriend seemed remarkably sober, and the obvious thought boomeranged back to me that she knew her way around the whisky bottle. Drunk or sober, she was wearing impossibly high heels, great for dancing, but no good for walking to

Princes Street. I had a solitary half-crown in my pocket as I hailed a taxi heading into town.

"Will you take this young lady back to the taxi rank in Hanover Street for half a crown? It's all I have."

The bargain was struck, and Miss USA disappeared from my life.

Discovering Edinburgh

English people from the Potteries tended to assume that Britain was a homogenous whole, more or less the same everywhere. To a limited extent, this was true, but the separateness of Scotland and the uniqueness of Edinburgh only became apparent slowly. It was not just the proliferation of Scottish banknotes that proclaimed difference; the whole look of the suburbs reminded me of my pre-war childhood. On every important suburban street, there would be at least one bank, maybe more, at least one bakery, maybe more, at least a butcher, a greengrocer and a post office. Above all, there would be a place of religious worship.

Life was comfortable and well arranged, not only for the middle classes but also for the multitude of tenement dwellers whose tall buildings lined the central city streets in faint imitation of the upper-class dwellings in the New Town. Edinburgh people accepted that their home should be one of a stack, with the best flats on the ground or garden level and the cheaper ones up to ten or twelve steep stairs.

The young man from the Potteries quickly learned that the pubs in the tenement streets were places where a man went to drink and not to enjoy himself. With the exception of the 'Sheep Heid', there was not one that would serve food either hot or cold. Going up the scale, restaurants in Edinburgh were limited to a tight central area based on Princes Street.

Religious observance dominated Sunday, but unlike France, the afternoon and evening were dull too. It appealed to an undergraduate sense of humour to attend the Rose Street Baptist Chapel on 'dookin' night', when candidates for adult baptism underwent total immersion in a large tank set in the floor of the main aisle. As those to be immersed wore a white nightie for the occasion, their wet body shone through the transparent gown, providing great titillation for male and female onlookers alike.

Another Sunday diversion was to attend the Highland Gaelic Church of St John in the Lawnmarket. The singing was wild and weird, like something out of the Stone Age, but strange and beautiful. Music was not a display item in the Church of Scotland, but they made up for it by offering a good protein-free breakfast on Sunday morning.

Things were already changing, but in 1957, there was enough left of the old ways to make the stranger from England keenly aware that Edinburgh and Scotland were different in a way that made them both unique, even slightly foreign. For example, the religious joke was a new area to be explored. Like female nudity, in the Potteries, it was known but not displayed. There were genuinely funny religious jokes, like:

"The Lord God in His all-knowing kindness was looking down into the pit of Purgatory where the souls in torment were wailing and screaming:

"'Lord, Lord forgive us for we didna ken.'

"And the Lord looked down smiling sweetly, saying:

"'Well, ye ken the noo'."

As religious animosity down South was a thing from the history books in 1957, the significance of the rather jolly air called 'The Sash' completely escaped me when I heard it wafted on piano notes that came tumbling down the steps of the Men's Union one afternoon. The commissionaire on the door said tersely: "There's going to be trouble in the basement bar, so stay out. Some of these b****y Orangemen want to prove themselves big men, so they're looking for a fight."

There were numerous keenly religious students, many of whom looked forward to a career (or calling) in the Church of Scotland. A certain number of these were clearly destined for great things, and some were pure nut cases. There were medical students among the dedicated and most of these lived in the Medical Missionary Society's residence for men and women. Married people were preferred as missionaries, and so this accommodation served a dual role.

Religion was still serious stuff in the Edinburgh in 1957.

A New Female Interest

There was a pet shop at the corner of Salisbury Road in Newington. I passed it every day as I walked to the medical school. A very appealing golden hamster was playing in the window display. On impulse, it became mine.

The pet shop girl was vastly inexperienced in gender assignment, so it became simply Wee Goldie. It made itself at home in my bedroom, at the back of my chest of drawers. So long as there was a small pot of water and a few orange skins on the window ledge, it was content.

I came back to my darkened room on the following Saturday night and put my foot into a mousetrap. On the table lay a note from the room cleaner: "Mr Duncan, There is a mouse in this room, so I have set a trap. The rodent officer has been informed."

The hamster would have to go. Casting around, I remembered that an American Baptist minister had casually invited me and Al Harvey, one of the six medical students queuing on the Dean's covered stairway, to come round for tea on Sunday afternoon. He had two children of primary school age. A hamster should be just the right thing for them.

I put the wee thing into my jacket pocket. Al and I rolled up to the S household at three on the dot and were invited into the front room, with its fire, its upright piano and its dark plush curtains. After a cup of tea, I casually asked the little boy and girl if they would like to see something interesting. I pulled out the golden hamster with her big innocent eyes, expecting the children to stroke her. They never got the chance, for a glass-shattering shriek from Mrs S caused Goldie to leap out of my hand and scuttle under the piano. What a b****y mess!

Mrs S gathered the children and fled to another room, while her husband, looking a little white, asked us to take Goldie home. If you have never tried the exercise of extracting a hamster or equivalent, from an upright piano, I should warn you that it poses more than a little difficulty. It was Al who, for want of a better phrase, hit the right note by playing on the piano the only loud piece that he knew (sort of). After five minutes of *Thunder and Lightning*, Goldie rolled out from the piano in a semi-comatose state. I took her back to the pet shop the next day and got a full refund because (anyone could see!) she was about to give birth. The girl at the pet shop still hadn't read that bit of the instruction manual, so she believed me.

The Rectorial Election

Puzzling graffiti around the medical Quad urged the reader to 'Vote for Ken More', so I enquired the meaning and the occasion of the vote. I discovered two things:

First, there was to be a Rectorial election.

Second, Kenneth More was a well-known actor who had played the lead in a 1955 film, *Doctor in the House*, a potent recruiting story for medical schools all over Britain, despite being set in London.

This information still left the question open as to what exactly is a Rector and who elects him (in those days, it would definitely be him). Apparently, Edinburgh University held onto an Italian Renaissance form of governance, whereby the student body shared power in the Court of the Senate of the University, through a representative of their own choice. This Rector had the right to take the chair of the Court and to bring to the attention of the Senate matters of concern to the students.

Although there was to be a properly organised paper ballot, tradition demanded that it be preceded by a student fight between the backers of the various candidates. To protect the worthy citizens of Edinburgh from the scenes of rowdy bad behaviour involved in even a pretend riot, the University authorities ruled that it should be entirely confined to the Old Quad. Amid august classical surroundings, the medical students fought the law students for possession of the steps beneath the clock. This ancient timepiece would tailor the proceedings to three in the afternoon, at which hour its chimes would declare the winner to be whoever held the steps.

Looking back, the whole fight seems now to be incredibly silly. There was an unwritten agreement in advance that no serious blows were to be struck and no blood to be shed, so there was general mauling and wrestling of the type that can be seen on any Saturday afternoon club rugby match. Chimney soot was thrown; bad eggs, rotten fruit, blotting paper soaked in ink, every imaginable filth clouded the air of the Rectorial fight of 1957.

This pantomime fight suddenly became real when some idiot threw a broken wooden box into the crowd. Its jagged ends struck a youngster on the head and stuck in his neck like some weird missile from a science fiction movie. A group of students rushed to his aid and bundled him into the street. A passing taxi took the wounded boy to Casualty at the Royal Infirmary.

For me, that was the end of a silly game. I mounted a double-decker going back to Newington, only to be sharply ordered off by the conductress: "Off ye go, Jimmie, and get cleaned up. Ye're no fit for decent folk in all that stour."

She was quite right; I looked like a chimney sweep, and I stank like a drain. By the greatest good luck, my spare rugby kit was in a locker in the nearby university gymnasium where hot showers were always available. A cleaner, more lightly clad student soon emerged carrying a bundle of wet clothing wrapped in a towel. As he walked back to Salisbury Green through the Pleasance and the slums of St Leonard Street, nobody made any remarks about his cherubic, freshly boiled complexion.

The Rectorial ballot was so quiet as almost to be a non-event. The medical students had been proposing a former professor of surgery, but the arts students' candidate won the election. Ironically, their man was James Robertson Justice who had won fame for his portrayal of a fictitious surgeon in 'Doctor in the House'. He gave what Sir Edward Appleton described as 'an electrifyingly alive' inaugural address three months later in the McEwan Hall when his artificial pearls of carefully composed, literate and thoughtful philosophy were cast before an audience of real swine.

Medical students of the 1950s tried to conform to a stereotype of disorderly behaviour, quite oblivious to the fact that it showed them to be exactly what they were: silly, thoughtless schoolboys. Neither before nor since have I attended any public meeting at which a section of the audience behaved so badly that everything had to halt while they were ejected. The new Rector took it in good part, for, after all, half his theme was the need for the younger generation to make the changes that their elders had neglected to make.

Still absolutely relevant today, the other half was on the need to raise the status and payment of the teaching profession in order to save Scotland from losing its very varied culture with its ancient background. Government sanctioned parsimony, coupled with political disinterest, he felt, was likely to destroy something precious unless the younger generation took action.

The same speech could be made today to address the same problems. The same stupid reluctance to change persists and is passed down through the generations. Human attitudes change very little and human behaviour changes even less. Nevertheless, I still keep a copy of this Rectorial address, even now after having joined the older generation who are convinced that the country is going to the dogs.

Charities Week Starts with a Bang

The summer term was the third academic period of ten weeks and ended with examinations for the first year of medicine. With the calendar moving rapidly toward an academic examination that would decide whether or not they could proceed to the serious study of medicine, there was obviously little time to waste; so we squandered it in pursuit of an old-fashioned fantasy.

The first two weeks were, therefore, given over to festivities connected with raising money for various charities, a rather Edwardian conception that trailed attached strings of generous condescension to the deserving poor. Whatever the political and social implications may have been, this week with its dances and events was an opportunity eagerly seized by most of the student body.

Edinburgh students were very fond of torchlight processions, so Charities Week started with one from the Castle Esplanade to the top of Calton Hill. There, torches were dumped into a great bonfire whose blaze illuminated the setting for the dramatic launch of Edinburgh's first space rocket. It looked imposing as it stood on three fins and pointed its sharp nose to the moon. TV cameramen took views of the audience as they gazed at the silver rocket in the flicker of the festive fire. They all knew the event would be a student spoof; nevertheless, the TV presenter collared half a dozen male students, a group that included me because I was wearing a blue–and-white-striped seaman's jersey, a souvenir of France, which looked well on their black and white screen.

With theatrical precision, a countdown was conducted by a white-coated boffin type of student hamming it up in horn-rimmed glasses. As the red light for 'fire' came on, I was to signal 'get down' to the half dozen in front of the camera. It was just as well we did so because whoever had made that rocket had put one hell of an overcharge into its tail.

Instead of a feeble 'Phut', big joke, ha, there was an almighty

Flash Bang

As a hundredweight of fertiliser and petrol went up with an explosion, that would have made the IRA proud. Only through luck were there no resulting injuries.

The student crowd drifted off into the night or down to Poole's Dance Hall near Holyrood House. This rather scruffy hangout no longer exists; it has been engulfed into a vast hotel complex and so Edinburgh boy must now encounter Edinburgh girl on Facebook or some other electronic website.

Charities collection boxes went out from The Charities office in the Old Quad to all four of the official student residences and to hundreds of groups of students in bed-and-breakfast lodgings. It surprised me how pleasantly the people of the town joined in the fun; how eagerly they pressed silver coins into our collection tins and how little rancour there was displayed at the antics of gilded youths gathering money from the not very well off. Perhaps we were nicer people in those days, or maybe full employment had brought a truce to class warfare.

Prestonfield House

Entering into the spirit of the occasion meant taking a collection tin around the tenements on Dalkeith Road. As the spring evening, light began to fail, and after many tenements, there remained a solitary way up a winding tree-lined driveway. Its end revealed the approach to a great house, a secluded stone Jacobean Manor. Long yellow rectangles of light fell out of a dozen ground floor windows, illuminating the surrounding lawns and making the encircling trees black by contrast.

This was 'Prestonfield House', an upmarket hotel, set among tall elms planted in the shape of an ace of clubs. This arrangement was chosen by a seventeenth-century owner who claimed to have won the Prestonfield estate on the turn of a card—the ace of clubs.

Clearly, it was not simply a matter of walking into a hotel dining room and rattling a collection can. This was a matter that called for diplomatic skills. The first thing was to speak to the manager; he must have endured Charities Week many times.

The front entrance to this posh hotel was guarded by the sandstone columns of a coach porch, left over from the days when the gentry would arrive by coach and horses. The outer door was of half-length plate glass, through which could be seen the red turkey carpets and polished wood of the reception hall. The problem that immediately confronted me, in fact, that looked me straight in the eye, was a huge Great Dane and his bark indicated that he was in no mood for polite small talk. Pulling a shiny brass knob started a whole peel of bells inside this menacing house. The barking increased. This big dog obviously was of the type that would not be content with chewing my leg: he wanted to tear out my throat.

A tall, athletic man dressed in town tweeds appeared behind the glass door. Grasping the mastiff's choker chain, he opened the door to the rain-sodden student clasping the big yellow Charities tin. The owner of the hotel took in the situation at first glance.

"Oh, you don't want to waste your time with these bloody old fuddy-duddies. They will only give you pennies!

"Here, I'll put in for the whole place."

Forthwith, he popped into my collection tin a folded five-pound note. Make allowances for the change in the value of the currency since 1957/1958, and you will begin to appreciate the magnitude of this generosity. Whatever thanks I offered then were inadequate, but they were sincerely meant.

Border Raids

Charities Week also included 'Border Raids', in which busloads of students, menacingly armed with collecting tins, descended onto peaceful towns in the Scottish Borders. Special permission from the appropriate authorities had been obtained in advance, so the Bank of Scotland manager in Hawick was not unduly alarmed by the sudden intrusion of ten persons dressed as highwaymen, pirates, wild Highlanders or mermaids. He took it in good part and duly put coins into ten collecting tins and bade us a hearty 'good day'. On their return from such forays, this ragged crew of pirates and robbers would receive free entry to any of the many student dances being held that night.

The Charities Procession

Saturday afternoon, with its student parade of specially decorated floats, dominated Princes Street for two hours. On these floats, there was displayed the best and worst of student wit and devising. Student invention seldom strayed beyond a desire to shock the elderly, so they tended to equate dressing up with taking off their clothes. Nothing obscene was offered, just a bit of lavatory humour.

As each year the Charities theme changed, being Chinese one year, French the next and so on, the prize for best float went to the one that seemed to the judges best to combine this theme with the main object of the week. This aim was, of course, to raise money for the University Settlement, a charitable housing scheme. Today, such lofty charity is deemed politically incorrect, but such sentiments are often merely mouthed excuses for the tight-fisted and mean-minded.

The pirates manning these motorised ships; the bathers splashing water over everybody in the make-believe bathroom; the veterinary students pumping the tail of a wooden cow to get milk; all these shared the harmless fun of gathering a few coins by raising a laugh from the crowd on Princes Street. Neither spectators nor students could be bothered with the rigid politically correct rules that govern the thinking of mental midgets. They all hoped to contribute to the good of the community.

First Year & Basic Sciences

After Charities Week, it was back to work in preparation for the examinations in June. The first year of medicine was a course perfectly suited to introducing the 'know nothings' to the basic sciences. It was also brilliantly taught by very senior people. Edinburgh Medical School was giving its best teachers the task of validating the Dean's belief in the possibility of training non-scientific students to be doctors.

Coming to medicine, as I did, with a technical but non-scientific background, I had tried to prepare myself by spending the evenings of the previous winter in classes at the North Staffs Technical College in Stoke. This experience offered an illuminating exposure to inadequate, if not downright poor teaching.

By way of illustration, there is a mathematical concept in physics that goes by the name of 'simple harmonic motion'. The poor physics class at Stoke Tech struggled vainly for six weeks on six consecutive winter evenings to try to understand it. In Edinburgh, the Reader in Physics got the concept over in forty minutes to a mixed class of three hundred and fifty students. That is not the only example of the highest level of teaching that sticks in my memory.

The Professor of Zoology, Michael Swann, taught us one of the most important lessons of our medical life, one that has endured for sixty years. On a winter morning, he was in the middle of his 9 o'clock lecture in the zoology amphitheatre (yet another of the old Edinburgh design where rings of students are stacked in a semi-circle, high above a podium). The double doors to the lecturer's left suddenly and without warning banged open to admit a noisy procession of white-coated laboratory technicians. Banging tin trays and blowing hunting horns, shouting and singing, they marched right past the podium and out the other side. As the exit doors closed, we students looked at each other and then at the professor.

He said: "This is a most serious matter. Goodness knows what consequences will follow. I want each of you to take a clean piece of paper, head it with your name, date it and time it. Then write down your description of what you yourself saw and heard. Please leave your witness statement on this desk as you leave."

A week later, we gathered in the same theatre to listen to the professor.

"I have read all one hundred and twenty witness statements that you left for me, following that incident last week. It is interesting that none of you mentioned the fact that while the disturbance flowed through the lecture room, your professor bent down to pick up a half-full waste paper basket," which he then emptied onto the table in front of him. He next placed the empty basket over his head for five seconds before putting it back.

He continued, "Believe me, this is an important lesson in experimental science, and I wish that I could claim it for my own. Harvard Medical School, unfortunately, beat me to it by conducting an experiment with first-year medical students like you, and they made a film of the occasion that you may see for yourselves sometime. In this film of a basketball match between two teams, the students were asked to count the number of times the ball was passed by white players, compared with the number of passes by black players. Various counts were offered up, but nobody remarked on the fact that a man in a gorilla suit wandered through the game from one end to the other. It's very well known in academic circles and is often referred to as 'The Invisible Gorilla' experiment.

"The point made in the film, and the one I am repeating is that in the experiment, we tend unconsciously to discard as irrelevant those findings that do not fit into our preconceived patterns. The whole point of conducting a scientific experiment is that we do not know the answer in advance. To put it another way, we sometimes ignore facts that are right under our nose because they seem irrelevant at the time. The unexpected, perhaps even the unwanted, may contain a discovery. Think of a penicillin mould dirtying a stored Petri dish."

Professor Swann belonged to a modern generation of university teachers whose lectures deliberately contained gaps which the students, even medical students, were expected to fill with a little reading around the subject. This I discovered at the resits in zoology, when the paper contained a rogue question on DNA. It had not figured in any of the lectures.

Quite by chance during the long vacation, I had been given a copy of the current Pelican publication, *Today's Science*, containing a very full article on the work of Watson

& Crick and an account of the double helix of chromosomes. It was both fascinating and easily regurgitated at the exam. Deemed to have passed the first professional exam, I was allowed to proceed to the second year of medicine, thanks to a paperback Pelican.

The Second Professional Examination

Pre-Clinical Subjects

We second-year medical students in 1958 were privileged to be ushered into the study of anatomy, physiology and biochemistry over the strong bridge of teaching provided by the excellent first-year lectures. Organic chemistry led into biochemistry, the anatomy of the earthworm and rabbit led seamlessly into human anatomy and physiology sprang out of a mixture of the lot. With the sole exception of biochemistry, the very high standard of teaching continued. The major change was that for the next two years, all our lectures would take place in the New Quad, the focal buildings of the Medical School.

The New Quad is a Victorian essay in Florentine Renaissance architecture. Rising on four floors of offices, classrooms and lecture theatres, the red pantiles of its roof, which discretely covered post-graduate laboratories, contrast sharply with the blue-grey slates of its late neighbour, the Royal Infirmary. Middle Meadow walk separated the two closely related institutions by a wall, a few yards of tarmac, a few trees and a patch of grass. From the medical school, a large Gothic arch doorway in our Medici palace of learning gave access to the side entrance of the Infirmary.

Those returning from ERI through the short tunnel from this doorway into the Medical Quadrangle, found themselves surrounded by soot-blackened stone buildings connecting perfectly on four sides. The main, wider ceremonial gateway stood (and still stands) diagonally opposite on the left, while a lesser arch faced the entering student, beckoning the way through to the Reid School of Music.

Male students frequently made straight through the smaller arch on their way to the Men's Union. It led to the nearest WC/urinal. Whether by accident or by spiteful Calvinist design, it is hard to tell, but the above pit stop was in a basement, the steps down to which were guarded by the bust of a former Archbishop of Canterbury, whose patrician nose is permanently wrinkled at the offensive odour rising to it. Other less elegant, but by no means unimportant memorials were displayed within the Quadrangle itself, notably one to Naval Surgeon James Lind, who in 1760 advocated the use of citrus fruit juice to prevent scurvy (due to vitamin C deficiency) on long voyages.

Unfortunately, this vital discovery led to generations of British sailors being called 'Limeys' by their US opponents. Another bronze plaque records the fact that the Polish Army School of Medicine was housed here during World War II. Above all, the New Quad was sternly, darkly impressive, and it contained our place of instruction for the next two years before we would be allowed to set foot in the Wards of the Royal Infirmary. For all of us, the first big hurdle was the Anatomy School.

Anatomy

In every medical student's mind before first entering the dissecting room is the dread that they might disgrace themselves on encountering thirty corpses. The sweet smell of rotting apples, mixed with the sharp tang of formalin seeped into the passageway where one hundred and eighty of us left our coats and briefcases on the black coat hooks clustered on both sides. It reminded me of evening classes at Stoke Technical College when the freshly scrubbed miners pursuing a Deputy Manager's Certificate through the tedium of night classes waited in a tiled corridor redolent of Pine disinfectant.

On a signal from Dr Inkster, the white-clad Reader in anatomy, the students were admitted to the long high room where thirty tables were grouped in two rows, separated by a long alleyway of about two and five tenths metres in width. Each table bore a canvas shrouded form and a prominent numbered disc. On the wall, there were lists grouping us in sixes and allocating each group to a numbered cadaver. Male students were separated from female students in the anatomy room, and males were not allocated to female cadavers.

Looking back, I suspect a degree of Calvinist prudishness prevailed in the Faculty even at that time. It also emerged in the sex education talks given to first-year students by the Student Health Service. The subject of birth control was handled with great restraint with the result that, while STDs were by no means unknown among the student body, condoms were regarded as dirty barrack-room jokes.

I looked down the two long rows of cadavers, my memory waving vague shadows of my first day in Mechanical Engineering Machine shop No 1 at Stoke Tech. I remembered two rows of shiny capstan lathes and wondered where the hell to start, while the instructor, a decorated war veteran, shouted at the new intake of ceramics students: "Don't touch a f*****g thing until I have shown you how these things work."

In my new brown machine shop coat, I put my hands behind my back then, as I did once more in the presence of the dead. This time, we all had a copy; in my case, an old second hand one, of Cunningham's Manual of Anatomy. We were to follow in detail the book's instructions for the dissection of the upper arm. Some third-year students made it absolutely clear that head and neck belonged to them alone, and this was alright by me; they could have it.

The dissecting room used to be at the heart of medical studies, but by 1957, anatomy, while still firmly dominating second and third years, had moved more into the lecture theatre. Embryology and anatomy were taught formally by a brilliant duo of Professor and Reader who between them brought to life the study of the dead. They gave four lectures a week for two years, combining a great breadth of learning with warm humanity that contrasted strongly with the cold rags of human remains that surrounded the dissecting room.

In this butcher's workshop, medical students had the opportunity to fit in about three hundred hours. Very few indeed put in anything like this effort, but the 'hands-on' approach to learning suited some and, indeed, this for me had been one of the strongest appeals of the pottery industry. This formidable room also afforded medical students the opportunity to speak to the elderly medical academic staff who served as demonstrators, patiently pointing out the structures laid bare by the students.

One such was a lady of great warmth but of formidable appearance, for she had a steel hook in place of a right hand and her left leg was in a walking calliper. She mainly, but not exclusively, took under her deformed wing the women students and shooed away over-attentive young men. Unaware of her well-hidden sense of humour, I felt flattered when she brought a group of six women students to look over my shoulder at the piece of dissection that I had just finished. I was vain enough to be proud of my skills, which I thought were the object of her admiring demonstration to her female students.

Two years later, one of the women in this group spoiled my delusion. I myself had been the subject of the visit, during which these women had been examining the lynx-like tufts of hair atop my ears. Why the devil was this? Because she had told them that these tufts were an indication of virility!

The Professor of Anatomy illustrated his lectures on embryology with wonderfully coloured chalk drawings of the developing structures and folds of the growing embryo, leaving an abstract design of some beauty to be removed by the servitor who cleaned the blackboards. His lectures with their detailed drawings were not yet in print, so close attention and regular attendance were both necessary. To 'know nothings', like me, this introduction to human development was absolutely fascinating and helped me make sense out of the disorderly tangle of tissues that presented itself on the dissecting table.

A most unusual Edinburgh academic, the Professor of Anatomy actually liked the young people he was teaching. In token of this but also because he was comfortable in its clubby atmosphere, he continued for many years to serve on the

Senior Committee of Management of the Men's Union. The Men's Union, that Scottish Baronial pastiche of the nearby Royal Infirmary, was the social focus of life for those deracinated male students who hailed from outside Edinburgh. It provided newspapers in the reading room, a cafeteria, a white linen restaurant, a bar, four full-size billiard tables, a fives court, a dance hall on Saturdays and a library for the serious student. The Men's Union was its own little world and enforced its own discipline.

You may well have wondered why it was not just The Union, as it is nowadays everywhere. That was the whole point. The University had for years neglected the provision of adequate facilities for women. It also had failed to face up to the fact that the student body was growing larger every year and that fewer and fewer students lived comfortably at home in the cosy suburbs of Edinburgh. The Senate was in bad odour with the Universities Grants Commission for having done so little to provide Union facilities (an OK word for a social club) for the students at Edinburgh.

The University had then nothing to do with the Men's Union, which was completely independent. It had been built in 1884 with money raised over several years by the male undergraduates and graduates and jealously guarded its independence as a club for gentlemen.

The University had indeed provided a small Union/club for women in George Square, a mixed-sex coffee room in the Old Quadrangle and a mixed-sex cafeteria with a lounge at The King's Science Buildings, out at the edge of town. There was no coordination to these rather begrudging and low key ventures; mere sops to the discontented. The Men's Union charged a membership fee, but the others were free, though inadequate. Many students, not only women, therefore were obliged or preferred to make their own arrangements for lunch. There was, as a result, little cohesion in the student body at Edinburgh.

Admittedly, the members of the Student Representative Council paraded in their red gowns to attend a service at St Giles High Church (one was not supposed to call it a cathedral, though it undoubtedly is and was). It was hard, though, even for undergraduates, to take these representatives seriously or to detect any contribution that they might make to student unity. The faculties tended to keep separate, indeed, a rather tribal situation prevailed. The Men's Union provided the only unifying meeting space. This primitive arrangement had attracted the disapproval of the Universities Grants Commission and could not be allowed to persist in 1958.

The Men's Union Battle

Edinburgh University has had a strong medical connection since 1690 and since 1719 with anatomy, through the chair of anatomy, held by Alexander Munro Primus, then his son, Munro Secundus, and then his grandson, Munro Tertius.

This all-male tradition in medicine was only slightly dented at the end of the nineteenth century by the admission of one or two women. The overwhelmingly male student body at that time wanted something like an exclusive club, that sort of thing being popular among the well to do Victorians. The coffee shops and public houses of their grandfathers were no longer good enough for a more prosperous generation.

Through their own fund-raising efforts, the men of the University had been able to commission a splendid Scottish Baronial Union building adjacent to the Medical School. It opened in 1884 and was still running under undergraduate management a hundred years later. That is actually a simplification because there were two committees of management: a Junior Committee of undergraduates, and a Senior Committee of middle-aged academics, lawyers and clinicians. Together, these committees delegated to a retired army major the day-to-day management of a large staff of cooks, cleaners, barmen (men because drunken youngsters can be violent) and commissionaires (these ex-servicemen wore a uniform resembling that of the Marines and were supplied from an agency called 'The Corps of Commissionaires').

The Professor of Anatomy was a long-standing member of the Senior Management Committee. He was also a member of the Senate of the University. In 1958, he knew something important that was being hidden from the student body but which closely concerned their welfare. A seemingly boring proposal by the University was entitled 'The Composite Matriculation Fee' and boiled down to all fees, including Union membership, being lumped into one.

'Including Union fees' was the explosive device hidden inside a haystack of boring and seemingly uncontentious proposals. A flat fee would be paid by one and all. The student body was invited to vote on the proposal. Being a modest and retiring sort, I was keen to understand more about this apparent simplification of our various undergraduate fees. Standing for election to the Students' Representative Council (SRC) seemed an obvious way into the discussion.

Upon asking the Professor for his permission to hold a meeting of second-year students in his anatomy lecture theatre to discuss the matter, he pulled me into his room. What I had thought would be a simple yes or no turned into a thirty-minute discussion of the Composite Matriculation Fee. It was a revelation.

The Professor of Anatomy released the bung from a barrel of thoughts that had obviously reached the maturing point. His words flowed in an unstoppable torrent, something like this:

"This is very important. Nobody is allowed to say so, but the University is in an impossible position, and it needs the help of the student body, specifically over the Men's Union. Unfortunately, the University is too proud and stiff-necked to admit this truth. The fact is that the Universities Grants Commission is withholding about five million pounds from next year's allocation because Edinburgh University does not and cannot provide Union facilities for all students. It cannot make this composite fee work because it simply cannot provide union facilities for all its students. It does not own the Men's Union and even if it did, there is not enough room for three or four times the number of students wanting to use it.

"The UGC will compromise only when the University actually makes union facilities available to all its students, both male and female. They will initially overlook the fact that these facilities are inadequate, and they will probably impose a time limit to enable the University to build something bigger, but the UGC demands immediate action. The University is desperate and will agree to any terms to get possession of the Men's Union."

At this point, the Professor reached into his cluttered desk and pulled out a sheet of typewritten paper. He pushed it into my hands, saying:

"Reasonable terms might be this sort of thing:

1) While the fabric of the building should be maintained by the University (and there are big repairs needed), the day-to-day management should continue as at present—i.e. Senior and Junior Committees.

2) Professional management and all staff to continue in post, but as University employees and to be entitled to pension rights. The Union shall not be 'policed' by servitors (enforcers of University discipline). Existing rules of conduct shall be applied, as at present, by the Junior Committee.

3) All students, male and female, should make 'an act of membership'—i.e. pay a fee, refundable at the end of the student year. This would simply be to try to restrict numbers until such time as the University could build larger premises."

With my fact sheet tight in my nervous hand, I was gently ushered out of his office and into the large lecture theatre full of my expectant colleagues. His concluding words were: "You have the University over a barrel. They can't say anything other than yes to reasonable demands but watch them: some of them are slippery as snakes."

With this background news fresh in mind, it was possible to steer my classmates off an irrelevant male-female argument and onto the more important practical matters of money and best use of facilities. I came across the Professor in the senior dining room of the Union, some months later, after the internal political storm had blown out. He was relaxed and laughing as he said: "Well, that went off very nicely, don't you think?"

It gradually came to me that this nice fatherly Professor of Anatomy might just possibly have been using me in an internal struggle taking place in the dark shadows of the Senatus. Who cares now?

This totally unmeasured jump into student politics had unwanted knock-on effects. I found myself lumbered with a place on many and various committees. By becoming a Student Representative, I had become a representative student, a convenient lump in maintaining the wall of sugar cubes protecting a quaint institution.

Inevitably, the Union became a major part of my life in the first few years and remained for many more years my favourite lunchtime roost.

A Member of the Union Committee

Being a member of the Union Committee brought privileges, such as the use of a separate sitting room with a small office for the Secretary and President and, above all, the occasional use of a private line telephone. In return, we were to perform as 'chuckers out' at the Saturday night dances (the Union Palais). This was all right if you were a big guy, as I was, but smaller men often found drunken students unreceptive to persuasion. Just occasionally, as on International Nights, the rough house became too difficult even for big young men.

One such occasion was French International Rugby Night 1959. Seven huge Frenchmen came up the circular stair to the Dance Room. A small committee member, who didn't seem to be aware that the team had been invited to the dance, tried to block their way. He was carried bodily by the crotch by hulking great French forward and used as a human battering ram to force open the swing doors into the dance.

Being more cowardly but also able to speak and understand French, I calmed the situation by bidding them an elaborate welcome and interrupting the dance to announce in a loud voice: "Ladies and gentlemen, please welcome the players of the French International Rugby Team."

So far, so good, but almost immediately there came an urgent message to please bring down to the committee office the captain of the French team. The police wanted to speak to him.

A diplomatic word in his ear and a few steps down a winding staircase led this highly athletic-looking young man to the tiny office of the Junior President. Two rather dapper Edinburgh policemen, both obviously Special Branch and both quite obviously too senior to be dealing with the Saturday night rough and tumble of International Nights, were waiting in the private office.

The police started immediately: "The manager of your hotel has complained that a barometer is missing from your private dining room and is presumed stolen. What can you tell me about this?"

"Ah yes, the barometer. We decided to test its accuracy. We tested it for 'Wet & Windy'. First, we all farted on it. It was no good. It doesn't work."

"Where is it?"

"The manager will find his barometer in a wine bucket behind the curtains."

A short pause ensued while the police spoke to the manager. On the phone, the senior detective looked up from the desk where the phone sat: "The manager says he's found the barometer, but it's dripping wet."

"That was the second test. We all peed on it to test for 'Wet'."

The policeman sounded very chilly when he spoke to the hotel manager: "You've got your bloody Barometer, so what more do you want? Good night!"

The Union President got out the whisky bottle and the two Special Branch settled down to talk rugby with the victorious French Captain.

Christmas at the Union

The Men's Union Junior Committee held an annual Christmas lunch, a very convivial affair, at which those attending were expected to sing one or two songs and to tell a story or two. In Potteries' dialect, I told the story of the fighting dog that turned out to be a lion and the story of the little boy who wanted to play coal mines in the cellar. Though the song did not come easily to me, *The Union of Students' Song Book* contained helpful suggestions. There was an Irish ballad, *The Wild Colonial Boy* and a Burns song: *My Love Is Like a Red, Red Rose.*

It is only when this song is tried that the singer realises what a testing exercise it is. I tried to prepare for the occasion by attending a few church services; after all, there was precious little other amusement on an Edinburgh Sunday in the 1950s. The song went down well, so well, indeed, that the following summer, some of the young men present around the table, when appearing as 'extras', suggested it to the director of a film with scenes shot in Edinburgh University. That is how the very same Burns song came to be in *Journey to the Centre of the Earth*. The singer's voice was far superior to mine, so there was not the least jealousy on my part.

Down to Work

Picking out highlights of the early pre-clinical years should not obscure the routine of term time, for these disciplines formed the foundation on which rested everything clinical that followed. Highlights are remembered, perhaps even burnished and gilded, but there were low points too. Thankfully, the human memory is skilled at hiding away the dreary and the disappointing, the boredom of a dull routine and the pain of failure. Allowing for this, these memoirs try only to pick out the entertaining memories. The rest can be taken as dead leaves to be swept away.

Physiology

Physiology was, for us, a new and subtle discipline rather than a mere continuation of zoology. Physiology was taught so brilliantly that the lectures were completely wasted on most undergraduates. The gift of compression is what marks out the extraordinary teacher from the merely ordinary, while the lack of comprehension is the badge of the untutored mind. Understanding comes slowly and is the reward of study, which was our reason for being in Edinburgh.

Once again in the physiology laboratory, male students were separated from females because quite a lot of self-experimentation was involved, such as relating fluid intake to urinary output, or taking samples of our own gastric juices. Great care was taken to prevent any physical contact between the sexes. Here, once again a matronly figure in a white lab coat took the young females under her protection. I suspect that she also had a role in the animal laboratory under the eaves of the Medical School, beneath the red pantiles, where the doggie doctors worked. This area was out of bounds to students, and we never entered it.

There were endless experiments with newly pithed frog nerve preparations that entailed scribing onto a smoked paper mounted on a rotating cylinder the wavering lines of the nerve twitches resulting from a small electrical stimulus. There were other experiments on living human subjects (i.e. on each other), which often seemed to entail measuring the amount of CO_2 breathed (or gasped) into a rubber bladder while exercising on a stationary bicycle or climbing one hundred stairs or running half a measured mile round the nearby Meadows. All these experiments were carefully observed by demonstrators, who occasionally had to sort out results that didn't fit or frog nerve preparations that seemed inert.

The lectures of the Professor of Physiology were brilliant, but it was all too obvious that his opinion of undergraduates was low and that even of post-graduates, it was not much higher. He was a teacher impatient to be called to Oxford.

Biochemistry

Also, impatient for this call elsewhere was the Professor of Biochemistry, whose name eludes me. He was not alone among academic staff in regarding teaching commitments as a damned nuisance and an interruption of writing and research. Together the departmental staff chased research clouds and reduced undergraduate teaching in their department to the point where one of the Senior Lecturers took it upon himself to organise remedial classes for those many students who just could not understand the biochemistry that they were being taught.

George Boyd

George Boyd is a name to whom I owe an irredeemable debt. Without his careful guidance through the maze of biochemistry, I and many others would have been forced to abandon medicine. His teaching made a major, indeed, a decisive contribution to my career. George Boyd was one of those rare teachers who could understand what it was that seemed to his students to be difficult.

He was already known throughout Western medicine for his work on cholesterol and its relation to coronary artery heart disease, so it was a surprise to his tutorial group when he disclaimed any further part in the anti-cholesterol trials. Patiently, he tried to explain to his students and to any physicians who would listen that coronary artery disease was a complex metabolic problem, not necessarily related to diet; that cholesterol, and indeed, all foods taken by mouth will be rapidly broken down in the gut to molecular fragments which the liver will reassemble into other forms. He drew our attention in 1958 to the many and various types of lipid and to the significant difference between saturated and unsaturated fats.

The remedial class ran through the winter of 1960/1961, at the end of which the group had written twenty-two essays and understood enough of what had been taught them to proceed to the fourth year of medicine. Our tutor soon became Professor Emeritus. It still pains me that he died before I could buy him a drink at 'Sandy Bell's' and thank him properly. I did write my thanks in a letter to congratulate him on receiving his emeritus Chair and now wish that I had said far more.

END OF PART ONE

==================

Part Two

Before the Clinical Years Start
Dean Village 1960

The medical degree course spanned six years and was a bit like a box of novelty chocolates: there were dozens of special flavours and every piece was wrapped in an examination paper. All these bits of paper had to be collected; if one were missing, the unlucky student would be sent back to collect it. In this way, I spent the winter of 1960/1961 in the remedial class, reassembling my thoughts on biochemistry.

The good side was that I bought a small flat in the Dean Village, a beautiful backwater in the centre of Edinburgh. It cost over five hundred pounds, all the money that selling my sports car had yielded, and it became my home for nearly six years.

Dean Village is probably the most picturesque part of Edinburgh. It was formerly one of many water mill sites along the Water of Leith, a small river running in a steep gorge behind Edinburgh's New Town. The four great arches of Telford's elegant stone bridge bestride the narrow valley carrying road traffic effortlessly across. In doing so, the bridge hides the Dean Village quietly below in semi-rural isolation.

This valley was 'discovered' and captured by our Regency predecessors, who ran private gardens from their high perch in Moray Place down to the water's edge. There is even a small Grecian Temple to Hygieia in celebration of the health-giving waters of St Bernard's Well. This notion had to be abandoned when the waters of the river became befouled by the sewers of the great houses in the New Town, but the temple is still there for visitors.

Quaint sixteenth-century stone carvings persist on some of the Dean Village's houses lining the winding cobbled street. Ancient, newer and very new houses mix there beside the river with its small narrow bridge and waterfall. No tour bus could possibly negotiate this stone chicane, so the red sandstone of Well Court, a mighty set of apartments, built for the workpeople of *The Scotsman* newspaper in 1880, was peaceful and quiet. This industrial connection caused Edinburgh's middle classes to regard the village as a slum.

This view was not wholly unjustified due to the presence next to Well Court of a skin factory where sheep pelts from the slaughterhouse were processed to yield wool for the weavers of Harris and leather for the shoemakers of Northampton. On the whole, though, and except on Mondays, when the lime pits were emptied of pelts, the village was quiet, picturesque and sweet-smelling.

Looking back, life there seems idyllic, and indeed, it was, but the passing years may be adding a little gloss to my memories.

A Winter in Dean Village

Some Tory MP, anxious as always to save the poor from the moral jeopardy resulting from state aid, had asserted in Westminster that old-age pensioners could be fed on nineteen shillings per week, so that seemed a target to aim at. Being a medical student, it seemed necessary to add a rider to the terms of this wager with myself. This budget was for food only and must be spent sensibly on a balanced and healthy diet. For a start, there were things that were unnecessary, such as sugar and milk on corn flakes or in tea, but citrus fruit every day was deemed vital.

There would be protein every day, so on Mondays, I bought neck of lamb, which was the cheapest but also the sweetest meat. That stew or curry lasted five days. Survival, rather than cordon bleu cooking, drove my routine and trimmed my budget, but I was never able to meet the nineteen shillings target.

I had already stopped smoking after reading in *The British Medical Journal* the article on tobacco by Drs Doll and Bradford Hill, my first personal encounter with evidence-based medicine. It seemed consistent to heed scientific medicine in order to turn a serious potter into a serious doctor. There was no money to buy beer, and lunch was dismissed as a bad habit. I went to the gym twice a week and also went running with the University 'Hares and Hounds' on Wednesdays and Saturdays.

With the latter, on a frosty, foggy afternoon in mid-December, I won the club cross-country championship by being the only one daft enough to run full pelt down Liberton Brae in the ice. Sensible athletes declined to risk their limbs on a hill that even the corporation buses refused to climb or descend.

Winter was warmed by the kindliness of the Director of Student Health. I consulted him about a skin infection one Saturday morning and found myself invited to join a shooting party that afternoon; he thought that I needed more fresh air. He owned a rough shoot over part of the Lammermuirs at Heriot.

It turned out to be a group of six very senior consultants and two very badly behaved spaniels. I surprised everybody and certainly myself by bagging a hare. This hare was duly allotted to me as my share of the bag and was the object of some concern among my neighbours when I tried to prepare it for cooking.

Those familiar with the task of cooking a hare will know that the first step is to remove the skin. This requires some thought and a large kitchen knife. I did the thinking on Sunday and on Monday went to Grey's the ironmonger on George Street to buy a large butcher's knife. This very large, very sharp knife lasted in the Duncan kitchen for the next thirty years.

With this Victorinox knife, the hare was skinned and prepared just like a rabbit for dissection in zoology. Lacking space in my tiny kitchen, I took the job onto the common landing outside No. 39 Well Court so that I could use the well-washed top of my coal bunker, suitably spread with the *Sunday Times* newspaper. A pile of fur hid the hare's head and guts; four paws were neatly arranged besides. Standing there with the skinned animal in my hands as my neighbours' children arrived home from school was a serious blunder.

They were horrified and ran up the common stair to their mothers, screaming: "Mr Duncan's killed the cat!"

I tried to retrieve the situation by offering the skinned hare to the mother in question. She refused, saying that they couldn't eat something that looked so like a baby. So it came about that I first cooked jugged hare, but only after another trip to George Street to find a suitable cookery book at the Edinburgh Bookshop.

The rest of the winter was cold, but the loneliness was relieved by several more shoots. This kindly old practitioner was yet another of those senior doctors who were interested in young people as individuals, rather than as part of an unruly group. He had himself been deeply influenced by the great Baltimore physician William Osler, a teacher revered both in the UK and the USA, who held that medicine was far more than a means of earning money. This did not mean that he was innocent in money matters, far from it.

One late afternoon, as the shooting party rested under a hedge, waiting for dusk to bring the wild geese from the salt marshes to roost on the high ground overnight, the good doctor spoke about his plans to build a modern and enlarged Student and Staff Health Centre. The Senate of the University was opposed to his plans on the grounds of cost and site planning. A year or two later, I learned that he got his own way in the teeth of Senate opposition for two very good reasons and one very rich backer. The site opposite the McEwan Graduation Hall had been gifted to be used exclusively for a health centre. The deeds to this site were in the kindly doctor's name and were accompanied by a cheque for over one million pounds, also in his name.

He owned both the site and the means to develop it and he did just that. It was an early lesson to me that few public bodies; not the University; not the Medical Faculty; not even the NHS are consistently benign and benevolent institutions. All are, however, accountable to the public and before the law. This is their Achilles' heel, and paradoxically, this is their greatest protection.

Winter plodded slowly to Christmas and the problem of gifts. I took my schoolboy stamp collection to a dealer who offered me peanuts for British stamps, which were still useable at their face value. I stormed away from this ridiculous old skinflint and went to the GPO with all my unused British stamps.

For current British stamps with a face value of twenty-two pounds, the GPO handed me twenty–two-pound notes and charged me three pence in the pound commission. There was enough there to buy a handbag for Judy, some sweet things for Mother and for Father a bottle of vintage port. Christmas was a golden light on the black shore of winter 1960/1961.

The dark November weekends were illuminated by one simple piece of lawbreaking. Having been invited to a Saturday night party by an Iranian dental student, it was necessary to find something alcoholic to take along. It was considered very bad form to arrive empty-handed on such occasions. Unfortunately, I had been hard at work on an essay and had left my departure rather late.

The party was quite nearby in Drumsheugh Gardens, rather a posh address. Nearby was Macbeth's Bar, very unsuitable for a Duncan in distress. Trotting up Bells Brae out of the Dean Village, I reached the bar just as the towel was thrown over the taps to indicate that no more drinks would be served. The barman probably took me for a policeman and refused to sell me a bottle of sherry. From the back of the bar, a woman's voice shouted: "It's all right, Jimmy; he's one of us. He's a Deanie."

The voice belonged to my neighbour who had refused the skinned hare. She supplemented her household income by working in the bar at night. Glowing with pride at being accepted among the villagers and with gratitude for the bottle, I ran down the street to find the party. My kind neighbour received the next partridge to come my way from the shoot.

There was no time to mope in Dean Village because the revision course weekly essays kept me fully occupied and forced me to read the set textbook. At the end of March came three major examinations in biochemistry, physiology and anatomy. Never had I been so well prepared and never did the resulting passes delight a student more. I rang my future wife at LSE in London to give her the good news.

She said: "That's great! I'm going to buy a wedding dress."

Arrangements were made for our wedding to take place in the parish church at Keele, Judith being a spinster of that parish. We went to Hanley to buy a ring at Pidducks, the largest jeweller in Stoke-on-Trent. The bus conductor on the PMT (Potteries Motor Traction) red double-decker between Newcastle and Hanley gave my pretty little 'daughter' a half fare. I was sufficiently hard up to accept his genial joke.

Things Happen in Between as Well

With winter away and spring in full flower, the summer term of 1961 was a time for enjoying life, for rejoicing, for dancing on the tables and for entering into the Clinical Years. The nightmarish barrier of the examinations at the end of the third year had been crossed, though at the cost of thirty per cent of my former classmates. The future, by comparison with the three pre-clinical years, looked very hopeful. Best of all, we had six months to be normal people.

The Car Hire Trade

That summer term saw my grant restored and my clinical teaching resume. The big problem was that Judith was in London, while I was four hundred miles away in Edinburgh. There was an upmarket car hire firm with an office in Randolph Crescent, a place that I passed every day on my walks to and from the Medical School.

Classmates who had worked as drivers during the vacations had said there were nearly always cars to be returned to their base in London. They were right. Somebody like me, willing to work the occasional job on an informal basis, suited this cash in hand, rather irregular trade just fine. It just so worked out that there was often a big Ford or a big Vauxhall to be returned to Notting Hill on a Thursday or Friday.

The overnight returns trade introduced me to the old A1 in all its menacing dreariness. This was before any motorways were built, so the wise driver marked out the overnight filling stations on his road map. Paper maps were necessary in case of unplanned diversions because the road signs were often unhelpful, and it was easy for the novice driver to get lost. It also helped to know which of the transport caffs were reliable but, in case of doubt, one looked for big clusters of parked lorries.

The 'greasy spoons' were best avoided; they often lacked a toilet, with the result that their rear premises stank of urine and rotting cabbage. After a few runs, I had identified a couple of really big transport 'pull-ins' and though the quality of their cooking was rather less than 'cordon bleu', the quantity more than compensated their overnight customers.

I had had a word of advice from the office manager before leaving Randolph Crescent, to the effect that on no account should I carry a passenger. It appeared that the A1 wayside was strewn with dodgy characters who regarded hire cars as easy prey. As a result, the careful driver should always lock the car before leaving it, even if, or especially if it was only to pay for petrol. The remarkable thing was that he was right. I was approached at every transport caff by scruffy individuals, some of them female, looking for a lift along the road.

The garage at Notting Hill was easy to find, though I cannot remember why. The target was to deliver the car by 7 o'clock in the morning so that it could be cleaned and readied for the next hire at 9:00. That was when I got paid and had to hand over the unused petrol tokens (not cash). Once they had given me my cash and the train fare to Edinburgh, I would enquire about returns to the Edinburgh depot, and often enough there was one. The same terms would apply: fifteen quid plus train fare; only, I wouldn't be needing a London train fare, would I? Presumably, that money went into the office manager's back pocket.

On one memorable Saturday, the Irish manager at Notting Hill proposed that I stay available to go with him that afternoon to tow in a car from Reading. Special extra fee! To pass the time, I went for a look around the Portobello Road Market. There was a wonderful pub there called 'The Sun in his Glory'. It radiated cheerful hospitality in the Dickensian tradition, so I went in for a drink and soon found myself in friendly conversation with a group of rather older men.

Strange to relate, they too had an interest in car deliveries. They cut up a bit rough when they found that they were talking to scab labour who was undercutting their daily wage and taking the bread out of the mouths of their children.

Obviously, it was time to play the hard-luck card, explaining that I had been forced to live on my savings for nine months because there was no dole for students who fail their exams. They even bought me a pint on that!

The afternoon did not go quite so smoothly. The manager of the depot had decided to take the big Ford to Reading as a tow car because it had a towing bracket for a caravan. This, presumably, was the car that I was later to take back to Edinburgh. It was the biggest and most reliable car in his garage, so he said.

One more thing. He was taking along as a companion a rather hawkish female submanager. Her black hair was short and shiny, giving her a somewhat Spanish appearance. Red fingernails were her only concession to make up, but added to her feline, predatory air. She struck me as being a hard-bitten piece, and she probably was. The manager thought he was softening her up for seduction, and she was obviously keen for him to succeed. We drove to Reading in an atmosphere heavy with sexual innuendo.

On a garage forecourt in Reading, we identified the malfunctioning hire car, another big Ford, identical with the one he was driving. There was something wrong with this car's automatic system but whatever it was couldn't be fixed at the roadside, and it would not respond to pushing or towing.

The tow rope was long just in case the dead car was slow to stop. We tried the brakes before venturing out of the forecourt. Everything seemed good, though the engine would not fire; anyway, off we went. One of the rules when towing a car is that the car behind should keep the tow rope fairly taunt to avoid sudden jerks and that the rear car should do the braking, especially downhill.

All went well until we got into Central London. This place, on a Saturday afternoon, is not the friendliest of traffic environments. At one of the great intersections, I had to let the tow line lie flat on the road so that traffic from my left could pass through. Just as the tow car in front started from the lights, and the line sprang tight, a damn great double-decker decided to dash across the gap.

There was a BANG.

My Ford Zephyr jerked forward and stopped, its nose a mere two inches from the golden letters 'London Transport' printed on the side of the red double-decker. A policeman waved the bus through and ordered me to 'shift my a**e' away from the intersection. The only way to do this was to use the starter as an electric motor and the big Ford oozed its way across the square to join the others on the side of the road a few yards away.

The tow car had lost a portion of its rear bodywork, including the tow bar. Not the least perturbed, with a rejigged the tow line, off we went again. The policeman went back to sorting the traffic through this rather difficult bit of hand-knitted road. I now had no car to take back to Edinburgh and would clearly have to go by train.

I returned to 'The Sun in His Glory' with the boss man and La Passionaria. We had a few drinks, and with the greatest difficulty, I extracted from him the price of my life—five pounds. The last train from Kings Cross was at 6:00, so I left the two scallywags mooning at each other and went to the nearest Tube. That was the end of delivering cars by starlight.

Yet More Gaps, with Weddings and Honeymoons

Wedding presents slowly accumulated at the bride's home, but my savings were pitifully inadequate to buy us anything special as a honeymoon. Then along came a very generous present from my Godfather in Berlin. He proposed to take a holiday in Madeira, so we could have his nice central flat in Berlin-Charlottenburg for three weeks. A cheap return flight Gatwick-Berlin-Gatwick was purchased through the Students' Travel agency and that seemed a very neat solution.

A closer survey of foreign affairs would have been wise because Russia was getting more and more agitated about the steady stream of people leaving Eastern Germany through Berlin. This, predictably, reached a crisis point during our holiday.

There was a short ceremony in the very ideal of a country church. The thing that I remember most clearly was that the approaching bride was heralded by a cloud of brandy vapour. Later, the wedding party was decanted into cars and taxis and departed for a meal at 'The Wheat Sheaf' in Onnerley.

93

I remembered this country pub from my greener days. It was there that years before, Tim Showan and I had sought shelter from a black and unforgiving winter storm that made our battered car shudder and wobble. The old bar was sheltered to a dozen or so village men, huddled in the dim light of a hurricane lantern. Quietly, we had all listened to the radio on the bar as the US heavyweight demolished the British champion. Since that miserable night, the 'Wheat Sheaf' had changed hands and been very extensively modernised, moving up market from village pub to restaurant for the nice people.

We departed the church to the cheers of hundreds lining the main street of Keele. That sounds all the better for being undeniably true. The full truth is that this crowd were mostly Irish labourers employed on the building of the nearby M6 motorway; it was 12:30 noon on Saturday and the men were desperate to get across the road to the village pub, which stood immediately beside the church.

"Good luck," they shouted. Perhaps some instinct told them that we were going to need it!

Taking advantage of my delicate and exposed position as a newly married groom on honeymoon, my brother had given me a pink silk tie as a going-away present, little knowing that this is or was the colour of the Thames Leander Rowing Club. This, and the fact that Regatta Week had just finished, must have accounted for the great fuss made of us by the head waiter at the Red Lion hotel in Henley where we spent a couple of nights on our way to Gatwick Airport.

Our flight to Berlin was cancelled at the last minute and held over until 8:00 the next morning. This was a foretaste of the muddled and off-handed way that small-time airlines dealt with cheap fare passengers. I now suspect that the US Government was flying as many refugees as possible out of Berlin to other parts of West Germany. To do so they would be paying very generously for all and any plane seats, bearing in mind that Berlin was surrounded by hostile, i.e. East German, territory, through which refugees from the East German Democratic Republic could not pass by land for fear of punishment.

Airlines probably shunted aside as many as possible of their economy flights in order to cash in on this lucrative opportunity. By the end of our honeymoon, the small airline had gone out of business, and I had to blow what was left of my savings on two BEA tickets to London.

Berlin in summer 1961 became a memorable experience, made all the more enjoyable by the presence of my cousin Willi. I had met him first in 1951 when he was a carefree young man, just four years older than me. In 1961, he was still a carefree bachelor, but co-owner of his father's business. As a boy of fifteen, Willi had been conscripted into the Wehrmacht and had fought in the siege of Berlin. He told us quite amazing stories of narrow escapes and daring subterfuges.

Eventually, he had been rounded up into a Russian POW camp and, as a young squirt, had been delegated to the most unpleasant work: 'the shit house commando'. Squalid and overcrowded, the prison camp, with its primitive open-air latrines, was literally a cesspool of infection. Inevitably, he had contracted infective hepatitis and become too weak, too sick to work.

The Russians thought that he was not worth transporting to Siberia with the bulk of prisoners of war, so they just threw him out into the street. Yellow as a canary, and surrounded by refugees in utter confusion, Willi had scrambled onto the roof of an overloaded train and made his way back to Berlin.

Willi and my Godfather lived in a large flat in Clausewitz Strasse, just off the Kurfurstendam. It was very comfortable, and we newly-weds lived in luxury. Every morning at breakfast time, a pleasant housekeeper turned up to clean the place and to do the laundry. Frau X, however, had a problem.

Each day, she travelled in from the Eastern part of Berlin because the value of the Deutsche Marks that Willi paid her for housework far exceeded the value of the East German marks earned by her husband for driving trains. She desperately wanted to flee to the West, but her husband refused to abandon his state railway pension.

Most evenings, Willi would take us out to a cosy but an inexpensive eating place. One night, I remember in particular because we went to an eating place in a large wooden hut beside a lake (Berlin is surrounded by lakes and rivers). There we had a large tureen of Borsch soup that was so good that we ordered a second tureen. It was only on our way back that Willi mentioned that we had been in the Russian sector, for Berlin was still divided among the occupying powers. He was right to mention it late rather than earlier; that might have spoiled our appetite.

Apart from this minor scare, Willi was a most thoughtful host who introduced us to his wide circle of friends, most of whom were of our own age, in their late twenties and early thirties. There was a scarcely concealed sadness among the young Germans that we met. They were very pessimistic about the future, mainly in terms of the cold war and nuclear weapons. Most of the men had served briefly as boy soldiers and still retained visions of air raid shelters and bombed streets filled with tanks and soldiers.

With other, more recent memories of how the USA and Britain had stood aside while the Russians invaded Hungary, their pessimism seemed fully justified. Certainly, the Russians could have snuffed out the other garrison armies in Berlin within hours, and this fact made the confrontation between them both more ridiculous and more serious.

Meantime, isolated from *BBC News* and from newspapers, we continued to explore the delights of Berlin. We swam and sunbathed on a beach by a large lake. We explored museums to find the image of Nefertiti, the wall of Babylonian tiles and the relics of Troy. We found ourselves in the newly restored Rococo beauty of Charlottenburg Palace with its splendid Amber Room. We walked up to the Brandenburg Gate, flanked by a Russian tank and a Russian guardhouse.

The Russian guards were very relaxed about tourists coming and going to East Berlin and even encouraged us to take photographs of their new city buildings. This all changed ten days later.

Willi introduced us into the Tennis/Skating Club, where British officers' families could swim in the outdoor pool or play tennis or just relax on the sunny grass. It was here that we first learned of the construction of a wall. Among these army families, there seemed to be no alarm; perhaps, they assumed that they would be evacuated before the commencement of hostilities. There was a worrying similarity to the optimism of the garrison of Singapore in 1941.

Against such a threatening background, it was comforting to know that our return flight was only three days away. Full of confidence as an experienced tourist guide, I rang to confirm this flight, as was normal in those days. The reception desk at Templehof airport responded with horror. This flight had left three days earlier, due to an emergency.

The company had contacted as many passengers as possible, and they were very sorry that some people had been left behind. Another flight might be possible in a few days' time, but there was no certainty. Keep in touch!

Tempelhof may have been West Berlin's lifeline during the 1947/1948 airlift, but something more substantial than a promise was needed to transform it into our escape route. After waiting over the weekend, we went to Thomas Cooke and booked two tickets to London with BEA (British European Airways).

Heinz, my Godfather, returned from his holiday and was surprised to find Judy and me still in possession of his bedroom. He put a good face on it and took us out for dinner at a rooftop restaurant in the centre of the city to celebrate our wedding. There the bright lights flashed off silver cutlery and cut glass, while the bourgeoisie of the besieged city laughed and dined as though everything was normal. But it wasn't normal, and this was emphasised for all Berlin by a huge explosion that shook the building and rattled the glass of the great panoramic windows.

From our rooftop position, through these windows, we could see a huge cloud of dust, yellow and pink in the ruddy twilight. The word spread around the dining room that the Russians had just demolished a block of apartments that straddled the demarcation line between their sector and the American sector. It was in their way.

For light reading, we had brought along a paperback edition of Arnold Bennett's *The Old Wives' Tale* and had been sharing it as we lay idly in the warm summer afternoon sun. There are scenes in the novel of the siege of Paris during the 1870 Franco-Prussian war. One particularly vivid episode deals with the use of a gas-filled balloon by the French Army to take people and dispatches in and out of the encircled city. Rambling rather despondently down the Kurfürstendamm after purchasing our escape tickets, we noticed some colourful reproduction prints of early flights in balloons.

They reflected our longing to escape Berlin by air and so; with our few remaining Deutsche Marks, we bought four of them. These were the very first prints to decorate the walls of our home in Well Court, reminding us of the part of our honeymoon that nearly turned into a disaster.

The Real Part Two

A new life began as I carried my bride across the threshold of No. 39. It was time to become a serious man again.

During my three months absence from Edinburgh, 39 Well Court had been fitted with a bathroom and a water heater, thanks to a very generous loan from Edinburgh City Council. The coal-burning fireplace in the sitting room had been removed, and the resulting hole plastered over, leaving a ventilator to comply with city ordinances. Inevitably, although the plumbers had tidied away many bags of rubble and waste, the installation resulted in dust everywhere and great blots of naked plaster on the walls where pipes and wires had been poked through. Getting the home habitable was done in several stages: three hours to get the bedroom clean enough to use, followed by a rolling programme of cleaning, painting and paper hanging over the next six weeks.

Within two weeks, I was admitted to Jordanburn Psychiatric Hospital, the main teaching hospital for psychiatry. This sounds dramatic, but the plain truth is that I had volunteered to act as a guinea pig in a clinical experiment—for money, of course. A small group of male students had volunteered to be subjects, two at a time, in a sleep deprivation trial at the glowing premium of one pound per night (This was the equivalent of ten pints of beer per night). It was being conducted for a PhD submission by one of the post-graduate students of a clinical psychiatrist who later wrote a book on the subject, entitled appropriately: 'Sleep'.

All decorating work at 39 Well Court had to be halted. Judy took up her post as lecturer in Criminology ten days after we got back home and I didn't want her to set about the painting by herself. The awful reality was that she was a terribly messy painter.

The Great Sleep Experiment

The psychiatrist, Dr Ian Oswald, explained the bare outline of the project, which was to test a proposition made by a team of psychiatrists in Boston that dream time in sleep was so important that those deprived of it became psychotic. Their experiment had been conducted in a large US prison, where, to break the monotony of being locked up for long hours, the prisoners would gladly make themselves available as guinea pigs. The Boston group had arranged for these volunteers to sleep in a special unit, away from noise and disturbance. They had slept with twelve continuously monitored electroencephalogram (EEG) leads attached to their scalp. When they dreamed, their unconscious eyes reflexively focused on the image in their dream and the EEG would record these rapid eye movements as REM time.

As soon as these dream time/REM traces appeared on the EEG record, the Boston psychiatrists would awaken the sleeper, so depriving him of dream time. After a few nights of interrupted sleep, the prison volunteers became very distressed. Our psychiatrist regarded this trial as inconclusive because sleep deprivation was well known to be stressful. The British Army had used amphetamine by the lorry load to abolish sleepiness in conditions of long maintained combat. In North Africa, he had dealt with the after-effects of this policy.

He wanted to separate the two main waveforms seen on the sleeping EEG: the slow, low-intensity waves of deep sleep and the tall spiky waves of REM. His proposal was to establish a 'normal sleep' baseline recording, over four nights. This he would later compare with the waveforms in the recovery period after four nights of sleep deprivation. The rate at which the REM patterns returned might indicate their significance.

This consultant psychiatrist was a very likeable man who, like nearly all the consultants of his day, had seen active military service. He always wore sandals, as a result, he said, of 'trench foot' from weeks of floundering about in the mud of the Libyan Desert. As he limped along the spooky corridors of the old psychiatric hospital, he expressed his distaste for the desert in both wet season and dry. What, it may well be asked, interested the Doctor in sleep? His answer was always the same: all the workings of the mind, mainly at the unconscious level, were the province of psychiatry. What better time than when asleep, therefore, to study the unconscious human mind?

He was financially alert enough to persuade the CEO of 'Slumberland' mattresses to supply two of the company's very best products for the sleep experiment. For years thereafter, Slumberland's mattress adverts could justifiably claim that their products had been scientifically tested and medically approved following EEG studies.

I was teamed up with a classmate and friend. After four nights sleeping in the 'laboratory Bedroom' with electrodes glued to our scalp, he and I found ourselves released into the town with strict orders to reconvene at 6:00 with the experiment team in the doctors' dining room at Jordanburn. The PhD writer was supposed to be, in effect, our minder for the next four days, but he found sleep deprivation too difficult to handle and became invisible at night after forty-eight hours.

My friend and I played cards and Monopoly endlessly. We played board games of incredible tedium. We did crossword puzzles from at least three major newspapers. We went for long rambling walks in the cool night air. We did everything that we could to stave off sleep.

Our salvation lay in food, a good appetite being only too common among young men in their twenties. We discovered that the kitchens at the hospital started to cook breakfast at 4 o'clock in the morning. Two thousand fried eggs were stored in hot drawers, ready for the patients to eat at 8:00. We ate fried eggs with new bread rolls at 4:30 and again at 8:30 when we could also add bacon and spread thick butter on more rolls.

If the intense boredom of these long nights became more and more difficult to bear, the days were not much better. We were invited to attend the daily teaching session at which clinical cases were presented to an audience of post-graduate psychologists and doctors. My minder kept poking me in the ribs, as, to my own surprise, I started to nod off after only twenty-two hours without sleep. Card games became boring, so I suggested that on night two, we should all go down to 39 Well Court and do a bit of painting.

Our minder could sit down with a book and Judy could lock herself in the bedroom, while Sandy and I dabbed a bit of paint on the woodwork. It didn't work out according to plan. At 2:00 in the morning, I found my fellow subject, glassy-eyed and semi-conscious, about to paint an oak blanket box, one of our wedding presents. He was gently disarmed and we set off for a ramble around the Dean Village and up to town. Our invigilator thought he would just slip off to his own flat to check the cat.

We walked aimlessly around The Meadows in the warm September night, and we both agreed that we needed something to concentrate our mind and stop our attention slithering like fish on a wet deck. I contacted *The Scotsman* newspaper and was invited to visit the printing room about 12:00 the following evening, using the side entrance on Fleshmarket Close. We all turned up for this as our minder was especially concerned that we should not reveal the contents of his experiment in case we spoiled his PhD by 'pre-publication'.

The Scotsman was just preparing to run off its final edition, so we were shown around the busy print room and saw the 'hot lead' print being typed by the 'Linotype' process, a thing now fifty years in the past. We were shown how photographs were printed in a series of closely spaced black and grey dots which gradually merged into a picture.

Our guide rather alarmed me by his screams. I awoke from a flash of sleep to find myself leaning on the naked blade of a huge guillotine. We hurried down to the loading bays of the newspaper: one on Market Street below the North Bridge for lorries and the other, beneath this, opening directly onto

Waverley Station for long-distance transport by rail. That visit passed half a night.

We walked around The Meadows for an hour or two, when I suddenly received a violent blow in my chest. In a daze, I had walked straight into the iron railings outside the entrance to Chalmers Street. My companion, meanwhile, was deeply engaged in conversation with a street light, to which he introduced me as his friend. She was, he said, the most beautiful woman he had ever met, and he urged me to admire her large Ascot hat. Then he too woke up.

Desperate for diversion, I spoke to a features editor for *BBC* TV. He was delighted to have something light-hearted to stuff between endless gloomy news clips coming from Berlin. The only trouble was that he wanted two days to notice to set up the interview, so the next two guinea pigs got the TV publicity—and a right pair of loonies they looked after only forty-eight hours sleep deprivation!

Serious Medical Students the Royal Infirmary Clinical Years Four, Five, & Six

Inside the Belly of the Pelican

A serious student enters the Edinburgh Royal Infirmary:

> A curious bird is the Pelican
> For his pouch holds more
> Than his belly can.
> He can hold in his beak
> Enough food for a week,
> And nobody knows how the hell he can!
> — Dixon Lanier Merritt

Take no serious heed of this bit of Edwardian doggerel. It is simply used as the means with which to introduce the unique buildings that produced generation after generation of doctors and nurses.

Over the main doorway of the great hospital, there was carved in stone the image of a pelican, the ancient symbol of charity, in recognition of its foundation as a charity hospital.

Beneath this image was the motto 'Patet Omnibus', which young wits translated as 'He's waiting for a bus'.

On entering the clinical years, medical students crossed a few yards from the medical school to the visitors' door of the Royal Infirmary. We could have used the great glass doors of the ceremonial front entrance, guarded by the head porter at his mahogany reception desk underneath the stone carving of the pelican. Most of us, however, preferred the quick and easy side door.

It truly was a different world, and we were now serious medical students. The old Royal Infirmary wasn't all that old in 1960, but there were already plans in preparation for another one. As is still the nature of these planning committees, their main function seems to be to delay the expenditure of any money. These plans rolled from one scheme to another for forty years.

It is likewise in human nature to suspect such committees of being fascinated by the burgeoning value of the site that has been entrusted to their care. Who now can tell what deals and bargains were involved?

The hospital itself was, like Caesar's Gaul, divided into three parts: medicine, surgery and maternity, with various speciality pavilions grouped like satellite principalities on the Western side. While maternity occupied a smart large building of the 1930s in the corner of this eleven-acre site, right by The Meadows, the elderly Medical and Surgical buildings of 1874 ran as two parallel corridors, widely separated but joined by a broad corridor, nicknamed 'the duodenum'. In plain view, they resembled two garden rakes lying on the grass of The Meadows with a garden hose in a lazy curve between them.

The surgical buildings rose to four floors, while the medical wards took only three. The lower surgical corridor was interestingly different and constantly abustle. It contained the kitchens, the central sterilising unit, a bank, a post office, a shop selling flowers, newspapers, sweets and tobacco and, of course, the locked ward for patients who needed psychiatric assessment.

All the other corridors were tall and airy, with large windows and shiny floors. The whole hospital breathed purity, fresh air and disinfectant. The spirit of Florence Nightingale combined with that of Lord Lister in their joint dedication to clinical excellence. This dedication, above all, was what the stone pelican of the ERI fed to its chicks, both nurses and doctors.

The pre-clinical years had been desperately hard work due to the slippery intricacies of Biochemistry, but having been three times through the whole milling turbulence of anatomy, physiology and biochemistry, the next three clinical years held no difficulties. This was largely due to my new wife, who locked me with my books into the spare bedroom for two–and-a-half hours every night. She would then grill me on the contents of my reading, and, being a fast reader, she was always a chapter ahead of me, no matter what the subject.

This had an immediate bearing on life in the teaching wards, where a physician would take the ten or twelve students allocated to his charge and group them around a chosen patient. A brief physical examination of this patient followed a shortened history of the condition that had brought about admission to this particular ward. Then the questioning would start. Student by student, we would have to respond to questions on the presenting story, on the physical examination, and on what physical signs we had observed.

Treatment and prognosis were discussed in a teaching room well out of the earshot of the ward. This question and answer routine was good training for real-life doctoring, when 'make your mind up' time comes hammering in at very short intervals, like successive waves on the shore.

Unfortunately, my fellow students saw my readiness to answer questions as overconfidence. In our final-year class graduation book, they noted my remark: "I always try to have an answer ready, even if it's a load of cock and bull."

Crossing the Middle Meadow Walk from the Medical Quad to the side door of the Royal meant that we needed to buy a stethoscope from one of the medical and surgical instrument suppliers who grouped themselves around the East gate. There were various types available, so students tended to buy whatever the bulk of their contemporaries bought; this was nearly always a bell/diaphragm from Messrs Sprague-Bowles—'sprogs' bowels', to we witty students. A tendon/nerve hammer was also considered advisable by the shopkeeper so, despite the fact that every ward carried a tray full of these things, most fourth-year men carried a short metal handle with a red rubber axe head in their jacket pocket. These tendon hammers were as much use as a toy tomahawk and were universally discarded after six months or so. The women never seemed to bother with them.

Here in the medical wards, as opposed to the pre-clinical classes, we were mixed in by name, rather than by sex. It certainly made the male students smarten up. After four years in each other's company, several pairings were observable, but in 1960, marriage between students was very uncommon before the graduation of both. Slowly, through the sixties, this changed to the point where a third of the class had married before graduation and another third married shortly after.

Fourth year consisted of lectures in pharmacology, bacteriology, pathology, medicine and surgery. As bacteriology and pathology included some laboratory work, their lectures to us were in the New Quad, while medicine and surgery haughtily confined themselves to their own lecture rooms in the Infirmary.

Bacteriology was taught mainly in the laboratory while the students gazed fixedly down powerful microscopes. A variety of staining procedures revealed various families of microscopic life that are hidden from the naked eye, and if we learned nothing else, at least we fully appreciated the need to wash our hands occasionally. As an additional bonus, a bad encounter with a totally blurry examination slide in the bacteriology lab taught me the importance of putting slides under the microscope correctly.

Due to an alcoholic Christmas lunch in the Men's Union, I had inserted my slide back to front. To make matters worse, I had told a cherry-faced junior lecturer to 'bugger off'. He was only trying to be helpful. The Reader in Bacteriology had noticed and quietly indicated that my Christmas essay on immunisation had better be good. It was.

Pathology was a coming together of microbiology, embryology and anatomy. It succeeded in being both compelling and scary. The student suffered through each chapter, fully convinced that this dreadful condition or malignancy was already worming its way through said individual. Luckily, we all survived a little longer.

Pharmacology was taught with great spirit by the Professor, who moved a little later to become the first Principal of the Open University. It was he who first introduced the multiple-choice questionnaire in place of an essay-based exam. Because he remained critical of the validity of MCQs, he still set us a written paper at the end of the year. Once again, as with the Professor of Zoology, our lecturer expected us to do a bit of private reading and left a gap in his lectures for a question that would pop up in his parting exam paper.

In the case of pharmacology, this was a question about the newly introduced varieties of broad-spectrum penicillin. *The British Medical Journal* had published a full account of these, just four weeks previous to the examination, and I had been lucky enough to read it.

Most of our lectures on medicine were given by Professor Dunlop, the Regis Professor of Medicine, whose lectures, although immaculately delivered did have certain elements of stand-up comedy. Repeatedly he bade us listen and try to understand, instead of wasting time with note-taking.

It was akin to being instructed in the elements of acting to watch Dunlop demonstrate the rudiments of clinical examination, but his female patients loved the close attention. In the spirit of Dr Joseph Bell who had inspired an earlier Edinburgh medical student to write about Sherlock Holmes, he made us look at the information that comes for nothing, starting with using our eyes to look at the patient. Pallor, stoop, nicotine-stained fingers, eye colour, squints, swellings, everything that distinguished this individual from the next was there to be seen. The same meticulous attention to detail distinguished his technique for the physical examination of a patient.

We were to start the interview by shaking hands with the patient, feeling their temperature, taking their pulse rate and examining the hand that we had just shaken for signs of nail bed pallor, or fingertip clubbing. In short, we were urged to usefully employ every second of the examination. In many ways his teaching clinics resembled an acting class for schoolboys, given by Noel (Mad Dogs & Englishmen) Coward an ultra-smooth popular English actor of the thirties, forties and fifties.

In the days when X-rays were reserved for hospitals, it was essential for the GP to be able to categorise and distinguish between the breath sounds to be heard in the lungs of somebody with emphysema or cavitating tuberculosis, lobar pneumonia or bronchitis, obstructive airways disease or lung collapse. Simple examination, done accurately and well can save a lot of time and trouble. Prof. Dunlop tried to show us how to make sense of what our ears were hearing by demonstrating which end of a stethoscope to blow down. (By the way, that's a joke!)

Surgery was always entertaining but mostly taught by a series of gifted Senior Registrars who would quickly join the ranks of our consultants. The Professor of Surgery, short of stature and short of temper, was nearly always attending conferences abroad or symposia in London or meetings in the College of Surgeons. His colleagues referred to him as the Visiting Professor. When he did find time for his students, the Prof. was of good value and the wise student would carefully read up on the subject of his lecture because it would certainly crop up in finals.

A Clinical Clerkship in Kirkcaldy

Before proceeding to the comforts of the fifth year, medical students were expected to spend a few weeks of their long vacation as 'clinical clerks' in hospital wards, bearing in mind that they soon would be applying in earnest for clinical posts as house officers. A classmate and I spent six weeks in a hospital in Kirkcaldy, which was beginning a reconstruction program in its large endowment of land. The first phase involved building a four-story surgical block with the House officers' Mess and quarters on the top floor. The medical wards were still housed in old army huts in what had been the garden of a splendid old house.

What nobody then knew was that this garden also contained the hidden and uncharted remains of an abandoned pit shaft. Years later, eliminating this potential source of danger caused Fife Health Board untold trouble and expense.

The residents of the Mess calmly accepted the presence of two new boys from the big city; after all, we were their passport to two weeks of leave. The leading light of the Mess at Kirkcaldy was a tall handsome West Indian who had been captain of the University cricket team in two very successful seasons. He was a well-spoken, very direct plain dealer and greatly talented. It was an open secret that he was destined for great things when he got back to the Caribbean; he fitted into the role of leader gracefully and naturally.

This was my first taste of mess life with its acrid flavour of persistent conflict with the management, it being taken as an obvious truth that the management was the enemy of the doctor. Unfortunately, it remains the enemy today. The junior doctors' mess was on the top floor of a modern four-storey building and could only be reached by climbing a large spiral stair which also acted as a light well. The architect who designed the new block had not been fully briefed about the number of resident doctors using the Mess.

There were, as a result, too few bedrooms attached, so more than half had to use bedrooms in the wooden huts of the old War Emergency hospital. We all ate upstairs in the new Mess, where the food was usually good. Trouble developed, though, a year or two later, when the management decided to install a coin in the slot hot food dispenser to replace plated meals kept in a warmer for those working late.

The food in the machine was of such persistently low quality that legend has it that the residents ripped it out of its fixture, carried it to the well head of the circular stair and dropped it down four floors. The resulting bang sounded like an explosion and the fire brigade was called. The management was a bit upset and did not replace the vending machine. The residents of the Mess simply continued to send out for 'take away' foods.

The Mess enjoyed the additional novelty of a TV room. Dinner was at 6:30. Afterwards, we nearly all gathered in front of the TV. Under the chairmanship of Dr Lunn, a committee of critics would review the evening's programmes. As there were only two channels, this offered little choice.

Often, we sat with the sound turned off watching a London audience of youngsters gyrating silently to unheard music on *Top of the Pops*. This programme was given the title by the Mess of 'Arsehole Club', and the game was to shout rude remarks about the dancers or musicians. The lack of music scarcely mattered because the band was miming its own recorded music; some did it better than others. Today, Facebook, Tweet and so on serve much the same purpose.

Evenings in Kirkcaldy were so dull that my companion, and I spent time in A & E in the nearby Orthopaedic hospital, learning to suture and teaching the locum doctor a little about pharmacology and ENT. He was typical of many overseas doctors unsure of himself and uncertain. Goodness only knows how he got his accreditation. His inadequacy yielded a bonus for we two clinical clerks when, one evening, a motorcycle accident presented itself as an emergency.

A red-haired orthopaedic consultant arrived to operate on the rider and was delighted to find two Edinburgh medical students available to assist him. Neither of us had ever assisted in an operating theatre previously, but here was a very experienced ex-army surgeon who told us exactly what we were to do. We found ourselves actually learning on the job. For us, this was an ideal situation and the patient came out of it well too, despite being placed in a bed in a rotunda type ward.

These circular wards were a late Victorian introduction, built on the proposition that all fifty or sixty beds in this circular arrangement were simultaneously visible to the nursing station in the centre. Unfortunately, this circus demanded that the nurses have eyes in the back of their heads, which is an uncommon abnormality.

A Witness of the Holocaust

As a reward for assisting with what turned out to be a very difficult femoral fracture, we two were invited to have coffee and sandwiches with the surgeon. He fell to reminiscing about his days as a young surgeon in the army. He told us about being with the first party of British troops to enter Belsen concentration camp and how shocked and angry all of them had felt.

The senior officer present had asked him, as the only person with a camera immediately present, to take photographs of piles of shoes and a mountain of discarded suitcases. To his amazement and considerable dismay, he then was put in charge of the initial medical and sanitation requirements of this huge mess of death, disease and squalor.

This orthopaedic surgeon was typical of many doctors, surgeons and physicians who taught medical students nearly twenty years after the end of the war. So strong were the bonds formed during the war that it was notoriously difficult to gain promotion to a consultant without a good service record. It was not nepotism, explained one consultant, just paying old debts.

In this way, Professor of Surgery, who had served in Burma as Brigadier Surgeon to the XIV Army, chose as his anaesthetist a doctor who had been an MO in Burma. He had been in besieged Kohima, a name that epitomised prolonged and savage hand to hand combat. Similarly, the theatre orderlies were very likely to have served in a theatre of war known to the surgeons using their services. These orderlies sometimes remembered inconvenient facts about their wartime comrades and officers.

Moving On

Having disposed of a series of examinations in pharmacology, bacteriology and pathology in the summer, we moved on in October to fifth-year studies. These consisted of a steady drumbeat of lectures in obstetrics and gynaecology from 9:00 am to 10:00 am, before returning to the wards for clinics in 'The Minor Specialities': ophthalmology (eyes), otorhinolaryngology (ENT) and dermatology (skin), interspersed with one or two medical ward rounds.

Teaching in the Department of General Practice

Somehow or other, somewhere or other, a term of teaching in the GP Unit was crammed in. This new unit had just received its first professorial chair and its members were desperate to achieve academic recognition. It was usual for the doctors teaching in this unit to speak as though the GP dealt with an entirely different type of medicine and great stress was laid on the psychology of illness. They aimed to treat the individual as well as the condition, and they were kindly doctors, but far too touchy about their position of inferiority vis-à-vis that of a consultant. They worried about status rather than about teamwork between hospital and GP.

None of their advice could improve on that of Ostler, who a hundred years ago said to his students: "Listen carefully to your patient; he/she is trying to tell you the diagnosis."

Creeping slowly, recognition came with the realisation that general practice was less a clinical speciality and more about the administration of a thousand details and the organisation of time spent with patients. Gradually, the GP was becoming an office doctor and leaving paramedics to do the emergencies that needed hospital attention.

As the GP teaching unit sat in the Cowgate at the entrance to the Grassmarket, it had to accept patients from two doss houses, a transport stopover and some of the very poorest slums of central Edinburgh. It wasn't my first contact with poverty or low-income families; there were plenty of both in the Potteries. It was, however, my first introduction to the doss houses or as they were called 'common lodging houses'.

The nice lady GP to whom I was attached, sent me to examine one of the occupants of the largest such place. At 3:00 in the afternoon, admission could only be gained by ringing a large doorbell at an iron-barred gateway. A surly middle-aged man shortly appeared and asked my business (well, that's the translation for gentle folk). He was in charge until five, at which hour the doors would admit lodgers as far as a well-protected porter's screen.

When my mission was explained, his attitude changed, and I was allowed past the desk. Behind the desk was a collection of truncheons and a baseball bat—tools of the trade, he explained.

The man (this doss house dealt only in males) whose condition was thought at noon to require the attendance of a GP, had changed his mind and would probably be found in a nearby alehouse. The porter brightened up and became chatty.

"We get all sorts here. At the moment (1963), our best customers are Irish workers doing the heavy engineering and excavating for the new Forth Road Bridge. They pay five shillings (twenty-five p) a night and get their own private cubicle. They send half their wages back home to Ireland and spend the rest on themselves. Come on up and I'll show you around."

We went up a wide stone stair to the first level, where two large rooms stood held apart by a bare concrete room holding eight WCs, none of them with a seat and all exposed to full view. There was not a scrap of toilet paper nor any shred of privacy.

"They often collapse in here", said the porter. "Drunk or full of drugs. They're very dangerous animals and you're a fool if you trust them for anything."

The large rooms were divided into cubicles of the most primitive sort, one metre by two, with the walls two metres high and a wire mesh bird netting over the top to catch the bottles and other rubbish thrown by the careless drunks. Inside the cubicles, there was a shelf bearing a stained thin biscuit mattress at a height of one metre from the floor. Underneath this sleeping shelf, there was a large collection of empty bottles littering the dirty wooden floor.

Those were the 10p cubicles. The 25p cubicles were much better: they were full rooms with an army cot bed and a lockable door, but still narrow and only two and five tenths metres in length. The washing facilities were down in the basement, where they shared the warmth of a boiler with the urine soaked mattresses that were being dried for further use.

The basement also contained two large black steel coal heated cooking surfaces. The lodgers could buy food in small quantities to cook for themselves. They were mercilessly ripped off by the management. A two hundred and fifty gram block of margarine (shop price 5p) would be divided into eight cubes, each one being sold for two pence (profit 11p).

Similar arrangements allowed the purchase of bacon and eggs at a steep mark up. The stink of vaporised urine from the drying room permeated the whole basement and challenged all but the emptiest stomach. Nobody complained. The doss house was run by a private company, among whose directors were said to be a senior member of the City Council. Critics might face retaliation.

Being a student GP introduced me to life on the bottom rung of life's ladder. Some lived there out of necessity and some out of choice. Begging in the streets had not yet been reinvented; that did not happen until 1980. As for sleeping rough, that was only done by the occasional refugee from the doss house.

Poverty existed in the Edinburgh in 1963, but it was limited and mostly associated with psychiatric problems. In the early 1970s, a government program entitled 'Return to the Community' began to thin down the number of people in long term psychiatric hospitals.

This well-intentioned measure, introduced by kindly and enlightened politicians is a good example of the Law of Unintended Consequences. There were far too few carers in the communities that received the most discharged people. Far too many people when discharged from psychiatric care decided for themselves that the community from which they sprang had itself been part of their problem. They refused to fit into neat administrative boxes and just cut themselves adrift.

Above all, where were the relatives willing to give house room to family members with whom they had only the slenderest links? It was apparent even to a student that patients with psychiatric problems would take up a large part of their clinical time as GPs.

It was a fairly relaxed year, with social medicine (formerly, public health) to keep us amused in the latter part. This was truly a Cinderella speciality, despised by all clinicians and too often used as the last resort of the idle or exhausted doctor. Nevertheless, public health officers were a statutory requirement in every town and had it in their power quietly but profoundly to influence the health and well-being of millions of their fellow citizens. An eminent professor taught this course in the stony splendour of the Usher Institute. I'm blessed if I can remember a word of it, though I clearly remember one of his lecturers who had figured in Lawrence Durrell's 'Cyprus Trilogy' as a young army officer.

Many of us chose to do our 'Normal Deliveries' during this relatively easy year. This boiled down to the inescapable requirement to have managed (under supervision) twelve normal deliveries of babies 'per vaginam' and to have written a short description of the process, including a progress chart of the labour period. These notes, contained in a special notebook, were to be countersigned by a senior midwife and certified by a consultant obstetrician in the case of these deliveries being in a maternity unit other than The Simpson Maternity Pavilion of Edinburgh Royal Infirmary. Caesarean sections and instrumental deliveries did not count, so the student had to compete with student midwives for spontaneous vaginal deliveries.

Most Edinburgh medical students seized this opportunity to seek out busy non-teaching maternity units in the English Midlands and North because it was generally agreed that it was a waste of time to hang around any of the Edinburgh maternity units; there were four of them and in all the student midwives would be favoured over the medical students when it came to normal deliveries. A popular alternative was to travel to Dublin to the busy Rotunda Maternity unit; they even had their own colourful tie as a souvenir.

A Diversion into Midwifery

For no better reason than that it was near to the Potteries, I made my arrangements with a small country maternity unit in Cheshire. A cottage hospital with five resident doctors lay in the same grounds, so, yet again, I became a mess member on tolerance. If this isolated country hospital had difficulty in securing consultant staff to join the single obstetrician, it obviously had even greater difficulty in securing junior doctors and therefore treated them like prize poultry: they were well fed and warmly housed. The residents were so well catered that a kitchen maid came up every morning at 8:00 am to take individual orders for the evening meal.

All the residents were from the Indian subcontinent, and one minute, woman posed a daily problem. She was a Jain and would eat no food that had been in contact with meat, even with the steam from an uncovered dish containing meat. Curry of some sort was served at all meals, so this tiny doctor took her meals separately. Even in the sixties, it was clear that much of the NHS was heavily reliant upon foreign medical staff.

This mess had no TV, but this was fine by me as I had brought along in my baggage three books on obstetrics that I was determined to read. I don't suppose that medical students still read textbooks: they are things of their own time and are thrust aside every ten years or so by the next generation of teachers, all anxious to leave their name on a reading list. Be that as it may, I enjoyed my books day after day in almost uninterrupted solitude.

Night-time was different. Night-time was when the black bats of Hell and disaster flew down to terrorise inexperienced and unprepared doctors and nurses. They didn't frighten the

122

older, experienced and fully trained who had seen it all before and were no longer scared of the dark. Nevertheless, despite all their training and regardless of their experience, doctors still regarded night work with loathing. This was due in part to an old fashioned prejudice against shift working and partly to an unwillingness to adopt a flexible working rota as part of a team because this entailed relinquishing a portion of their autonomy.

Babies persist in being largely nocturnal in their activities and most deliveries seemed to occur in the pre-dawn hours between 3:00 am and 6:00 am. This view may be a little skewed by the fact that even out in deepest Cheshire, medical students were still competing with trainee midwives and that it was just possible that the senior midwives decided to let their young nurses sleep after 3:00 am. My first few cases were all daylight jobs.

A certain selectivity about the cases allowed to me became apparent in my first three. The first one was a big hefty farm girl of twenty who, though she pushed mightily, simply could not deliver. Making a wide episiotomy did nothing to help and did even less for her comfort. After two hours of sweaty effort on both sides, she was exhausted and contractions fell away.

To make matters of incompetence worse, I could not hear a foetal heartbeat, even with my stethoscope. The SHO, an attractive Indian woman, looked at the problem and reassessed the presentation and lie of the foetus. She had no difficulty in counting the foetal heart rate and ordered an intravenous drip with oxytocin to stimulate the flagging labour.

This was to be an evening delivery, so it seemed, but by 6:00, the SHO had to summon the Registrar. He arrived at 7:00, having had his supper and feeling full of scorn for medical students who couldn't even hear a heartbeat. Having gone through another assessment routine and been rude to the nursing staff, he declared that he would use Haig-Ferguson forceps to deliver what he described as a large lump of Cheshire cheese.

The Registrar's attempts at instrumental delivery failed and by 9 in the evening the Consultant had to be summoned from home. I doubt that he had had much to drink at home, but consultants seldom appeared to enjoy being separated from the bosom of their family by night emergency calls. To be fair, night work appeals to very few, though there are some elderly nurses who prefer it because the money is better, the work is lighter and their husband can look after the children. In this small country unit we had an early evening crisis: the patient was in distress, the staff were exhausted and ashamed at their perceived failure, and the consultant was angry that his Registrar could not handle a forceps delivery.

The consultant, whose appointment in the countryside allowed him to lead the sporting life of a squire while earning a good living from his private practice among the ladies of the gentry, composed himself to give a professional performance. In view of the fact that a medical student was present, it occurred to him that he should start this lecture in chapter one by reading the patient's notes. A red label on the cover of her notes meant nothing to an outsider like me, but to the staff of the cottage hospital, it was supposed to be a warning that she was a diabetic. The Consultant knew that.

In deadly silence, he asked the Sister midwife to check the foetal heart. She reported it to be about one hundred and forty per minute. The Registrar was asked to confirm this before the Consultant applied the tin trumpet to his ear. It was obviously a serious moment. He looked at me, still clad in waterproof and gown and asked what rate I had counted. There was no way to retreat from my failure to hear the heart.

The senior man said: "There is no foetal heart. This is a stillbirth. I am not going to perform a Caesarean section with all the hazards to the mother entailed in that operation, just to deliver a dead babe."

This was how my first case resulted in my witnessing an operation that I never again saw in thirty-five years of anaesthetic practice with full exposure to surgical obstetrics. This was a cleidotomy in which the dead baby was literally broken up and pulled out of the mother's womb. It started by screwing into the dead head a double-pronged corkscrew instrument with a large handle, similar to that used by a plumber to unblock a drain. The skull collapsed and the whole disgusting business progressed from that to cutting the clavicles and hauling out each arm.

The mother, meanwhile had sunk into deep morphine oblivion, reinforced by the liberal use of pelvic local anaesthesia. The anaesthetist did not attend because, being a local GP, he was out at one of the farms attending a patient. The Sister's opinion was that she could do without yet another prima donna displaying tantrums.

The pathologist's report two days later was to the effect that this stillbirth was attributable to the mother's diabetic condition and that the babe had been dead for a week, possibly a month.

My second case had been specially chosen for me by the Sister midwife. This Sister was a wonderfully warm and human woman and herself the mother of five children. My trust in her was puppy-like. I had carefully read the notes of the mother-to-be and thought they were a bit sketchy, but that this probably indicated that there was nothing unusual to record. She was certainly not diabetic and my careful physical examination revealed a sound and healthy woman. There were two hearts to be heard: the maternal and the foetal.

As I stood fully gowned and gloved at the bottom end of the table, Sister slipped a full pail of water between my feet. She said: "This will be needed if there is a lot of liquor."

It didn't make much sense, but there was a babe to deliver. The mother seemed to be slow to achieve full dilation of the cervix, but then got stuck. The midwives urged me to assess the width of the cervix by hand and to find the frontal suture of the oncoming head. Once again I found myself unable to give a precise answer. I couldn't feel the suture lines of the skull; in fact, the oncoming head seemed a lumpy mystery.

Those who have been through the humiliation of being unable to identify something that is supposedly obvious to all in the room will know the relief that I felt when the uterine bundle delivered itself into my hands in one sudden rush. It was an anencephalic monster!

"Straight into the bucket. It mustn't draw breath," said Sister quietly with an urgency that did not invite argument.

That was 'no go' number two and did not count for the logbook either. My third attempt also had been chosen especially for me and this time everything went perfectly, at least from my point of view though not from that of the mother. She was a robustly healthy young woman of twenty who had been a nurse at the cottage hospital. Labour started at 11:00 am and she delivered at 12:30 pm. It was a beautiful little boy, but I thought his colour was poor and asked the Sister about oxygen, only to receive a sharp dig in the ribs and a 'Shush'.

The baby was a dark colour because the father was a young Arab doctor who had deserted the poor nurse. The baby was to go for immediate adoption, as was then possible. The mother didn't even look at him before he was whisked away to the neonatal ward. The midwives were only mildly sympathetic. They did not hold foreign doctors in the same esteem as the home-grown variety.

My second normal mother was aged twelve years and came into the labour ward with her own mother. This baby was definitely staying at home with the whole family. Grandma firmly proposed to treat it as her own. It was none of my business to ask about the father, but incest was at least possible. Life in rural Cheshire was like that.

The rest of my cases accumulated over the three weeks of my stay in Cheshire, with a couple of 'firsts', in addition.

I had my first midnight ride in an ambulance with the supposed function of a 'Maternity Emergency Flying Squad'. I say 'supposed' because in later years I went on very many Flying Squad call outs from the Simpson Maternity Hospital and they were a sight more effective than this feeble charade of one ambulance driver and one Maternity SHO. The case was out at a farm about four miles away. The baby was fine but the placenta was retained.

The mother, looking pink and well, was put into the ambulance, only to be pulled out pallid, in shock and collapse after a bumpy ride over rough country roads. The Edinburgh

Flying Squad would have arrived at the farmhouse with an anaesthetist, Registrar obstetric surgeon, and two theatre Staff nurses. That retained placenta would have been removed, and the patient given IV fluids before moving her to the Simpson for complete stabilisation.

The other first was, as a fifth-year medical student, to give an emergency general anaesthetic. This occurred one fine afternoon when the Registrar Obstetrician was holding the fort alone, while the SHO and Consultant were both away in the country villages doing ante-natal clinics. I was reading in the doctors' room, quite unaware that a seemingly normal delivery in the labour ward had suddenly developed a severe complication: a foetal hand had slipped down beside the foetal head and obstructed the progress of labour. The Registrar laid a gentle hand on my studious collar and urged me onto my feet.

He said: "You will have to give this woman a general anaesthetic. I'll tell you what to do. You just keep her asleep long enough for me to get the babe out."

It was no use protesting ignorance. This was an emergency whose compelling net drew in all available help without discrimination. I gave the mother a shot of intramuscular atropine and turned to look at the anaesthetist's trolley (a Boyle's trolley, as I learned much later). It contained two ready filled plunger vaporisers: one of ether and one of chloroform. There was a Schimmelbusch mask, lined with clean gauze; there was a cylinder of oxygen; there was a cylinder of nitrous oxide; there were various black rubber masks and some black corrugated tubing.

"Get on with it. Get on!"

I doused the gauze on the Schimmelbusch wireframe with ether and held it near the face of the, by now, very distressed woman. She tried to cooperate but the ether made her cough. A second wireframe was handy, so I soaked its gauze pad in chloroform. Very quickly, our patient lost consciousness and I eased the mask up two fingers to allow plenty of fresh air to enter her airway. I was icy cold with fearful apprehension that I might, in my ignorant uselessness, cause the death of this woman.

Then it was all over. A roaring little girl, wrapped in a white towel, lay in the sister midwife's arms. It was just as though nothing unusual had happened. My patient woke up almost immediately, laughed with joy and vomited a fish and chips take away all over the floor.

When the three weeks attachment was finished and my Midwifery logbook completed I had learned a lot about delivering babies, bathing them, feeding them and putting them into nappies. This exposure to life in the labour ward also turned me into a fully-fledged mender of episiotomies because the midwives made sure that there was always a cut bottom to be sewn up. I supposed that their student midwives had more important work to do. An episiotomy, a deliberately inflicted cut into the vagina and skin of the perineum, seems barbaric to the beginner (and to the mother involved) but the alternative is to risk a tear that extends into the bowel. That is a major wound, far too serious for a student bottom cobbler to mend.

The pace of the labour room had also made its impression; how things can swing in an instant from routine to life threatening emergency and how important it was to act quickly on these occasions. The importance of other things had also been shown, such as the extreme potency of chloroform and the wisdom of fasting before an anaesthetic. Among the shattered impressions of a schoolboy lay the belief in the overall genius of the management of health services. That so called 'Flying Squad' was downright dangerous, a half measure that encouraged in the general population a false sense of security. It did no more than paste new labels on empty tins.

The whole concept of a country cottage hospital maternity unit is initially appealing. Immediate and local protection with warming associations of friendly and well-known faces in modest surroundings reassures people. The greater hospitals still tend to intimidate and inevitably because they take the most difficult and most dangerous cases, their image is associated with pain and suffering. Nevertheless, a cottage hospital, to be safe and successful needs to be backed up by a big hospital with a full range of immediately available medical and surgical services. Pandering to local sentiment and to special pleading on grounds of accessibility and convenience may win votes but human life is more important than that. If the quality of that local service is poor, then penny-pinching will be self-defeating and end in expensive litigation, with accompanying professional humiliation.

I have still no sympathy with a vociferous group of people who assert without proof that home deliveries are safe because they are 'natural'. Natural was a much-overworked adjective used to prop up shaky claims in a sales pitch for an appealing assertion. It was a word used to discount contradictory evidence in an argument over childbirth. Delivering a baby in a ditch, enduring the terrible pain of an obstructed labour or watching that child die from starvation because its mother has no milk may be natural in primitive societies, but that does not make it desirable. Overstated claims for the natural still seem to me to be mere blind optimism that nasty things never happen.

A small dose of midwifery certainly shook the schoolboy out of me.

Back to Fifth-Year Studies

This very strange year spent among the 'minor' specialities also continued our studies in medicine and surgery. As we were a very numerous year, a fleet of buses was laid on each day to take us in discrete groups around the various hospitals of Edinburgh. There were some very impressive specialised units scattered around the city and we began to get some impression of the vast charitable endowment supporting them. For example, the City General Hospital sat in several acres of parkland, just on the edge of the Pentland Hills, themselves a preserved area as the water catchment area for Edinburgh.

With this wonderfully clean atmosphere, the City General was an ideal site for a hospital specialising in Tuberculosis, Infectious diseases, Renal medicine, ENT, Respiratory medicine and Thoracic surgery.

Our first visit to the Princess Margaret-Rose orthopaedic hospital for children was remarkable. This hospital, following the Nightingale belief in the healing powers of fresh air and sunlight, also stood on the edge of the Pentland Hills parkland. As our bus, on day one, pulled into the long, broad circular drive approaching the main entrance, we were amazed to see a magnificent grey elephant in a flashing bejewelled harness and it was standing on its head on the large grass lawn. The Billy Smart Circus was giving a free show to about one hundred children, some twenty lying in beds, some more in wheelchairs and a few just sitting in the sunshine on the grass. We medical students were not invited to attend.

As a teaching hospital, it was a rather intimidating place, run by a Professor whose bite promised to be every bit as painful as his bark. His particular interest lay in spinal surgery for the correction of the deformities resulting from polio or trauma. We were told that during the war he had been dropped by parachute into the mountains of Yugoslavia to attend to Marshall Tito's orthopaedic problems. He was not the sort of man that made friends with his colleagues, so he presided over a set of loose cannon surgeons, each doing things differently. There were no female orthopaedic surgeons.

There were several other little hospitals to which we were not necessarily taken as students, but which stood ready to absorb us as Junior House Officers. There were small medical and surgical units at the Chalmers Hospital, the Eastern General Hospital, Leith Hospital, Longmore Hospital, Deaconess Hospital, Bruntsfield Hospital for Women and the Northern Hospital. There was a small private hospital run by nuns, but it did not concern itself with teaching. The Royal Infirmary and the Western General Hospital together were father and mother to this large family of teaching hospitals.

There were about one thousand convalescent beds available at the Astley Ainslie hospital in the Grange area and the Corstorphine Hospital by the zoo. This ample supply of 'second line' beds was the reason that the major hospitals, especially The Royal Infirmary, never knew the latter day condition of 'bed blockers'. Emergency surgery was handled quickly and pressure on the wards was relieved by transferring to the zoo or to the Ghastly Astley people who were over the acute stage but still in need of care.

We students of the sixties were privileged to be trained in a medical school that was internationally recognised to be the gold standard for excellence. If we had a fault (which was terribly unlikely) it was that we were not sufficiently grateful at the time. We thought that our Seniors were just inflating Edinburgh's reputation when they said in 1964 that it was the best Medical school in Britain, if not in the world. A little experience in England and abroad quickly made us realise that they were absolutely right. Now we look around us at the politically engineered desolation in the NHS and know with certainty that we were lucky enough to spend our early medical years in the Golden Age of the Health Service.

In the summer vacation between fifth and final year, most of us tried to cram in some hospital experience with a view to applying for a houseman's job after graduation. I was lucky enough to get, at very short notice, a three-week job in surgical ward Ten at the Royal Infirmary. The resident had just gone sick with impacted wisdom teeth and in those days that was a big deal. The surgeon in charge was a great bull of a man, but a highly skilled surgeon whose speed was comparable to that of the Victorian greats.

He had amazed his fifth-year clinical students when, at the end of June, we were gathered in the ward to collect our 'certificate of progress', without which we could not proceed to the final year. One tall West Indian had attended none of the summer clinics but had instead absented himself to play county cricket in England. At six feet four and lithe as a panther, he was a frighteningly aggressive pace bowler, quite capable of intimidating the opposition as he snarled and showed his big mouthful of teeth. That summer he played professional cricket for Warwickshire and was probably the best-paid student in Edinburgh.

The lady secretary called our county cricketer into the consultant's office first, while the other dozen or so students nudged each other and sniggered. We just knew that this guy hadn't a hope in hell of getting his certificate. We were absolutely certain that behind that closed door, harsh words were being spoken, possibly including a sending down. But no! Our man, cool as an ice cube, reappeared holding the yellow piece of paper recording his satisfactory progress in surgery.

His fellow students crowded around, eager to hear what had passed between the surgeon and the West Indian.

"He just wanted to shake hands with the player who had made such an important contribution to Warwickshire's success in County Cricket. Nice guy. Supports Warwickshire."

Attempts at a medical house job for the summer vacation yielded mixed results. Starting too late, there was only a discard job in the Rheumatology unit. A precious and rare experience in an internationally recognised unit it may have been, but not helpful for the general medical experience. This meant that I had to do a Christmas locum in general medicine when everybody else was snug at home.

The unit in the Western Genera dealt with general medical admissions, but its main focus was on metabolic medicine. All a bit high flown for an ordinary garden sparrow like me.

Putting up IV drips on this unit was just as tedious as in any because, in the early sixties, the houseman had at his disposal a very disappointing array of IV cannulas, mainly big sharp things that cut out of the vein if the patient moved too much, or, indeed, at all. It was quite common for young doctors to try to splint these drip needles in place with match sticks and then to splint the whole arm to prevent movement. The only IV giving needle worth a damn was the Guest cannula, but this stainless steel device had to be specially ordered from the Central Sterilising Unit. Most night calls to the ward were from the night staff reporting a blocked or extravasated drip. Those early IV drips were a bloody nuisance and squandered the junior doctor's sleep time.

The old wards were a mixture of small rooms from a hospital of another age and, taken altogether, held about thirty beds in threes and fours. Together they produced a lot of work for the junior doctors and Christmas Day was no different from any other 'waiting day'—i.e. when the unit admitted all medical emergencies for the whole of Edinburgh. The first emergency arrived at 12:00, just as the consultant was about to slice into a large turkey in front of an admiring and gently salivating group of female patients.

The initial trickle of emergency admissions strengthened into a torrent that kept the junior doctors away from any festive food or even the thought of it until just before midnight. A group of assorted junior surgeons and physicians then formed a plaintive group around an empty table in an empty Mess. We were all exasperated at the management's callous indifference to our lack of food. Had this been the Royal Infirmary instead of the blooming Western, the Mess table would have been laden with things for a cold supper.

To make matters worse, we could hear somebody rattling around behind the locked door of the kitchens, where an evening meal was being prepared for the night nurses. A young Australian surgeon was exasperated beyond his elastic limit by all this. He picked up the telephone and insisted on speaking to the hospital manager. We crowded round to listen.

Having torn a strip off the young surgeon, we heard the manager say: "The kitchens are shut now until morning, so just make the best of it and stop whining."

The Australian said: "Look mate, there are twelve of us here and we haven't eaten for sixteen hours. As I speak to you I have a clear view of a fire axe in a glass case. If we don't get hot food within the next half hour, I'm going to take that axe and cut my way into the kitchen and you can stick my job where the sun never shines."

Twenty minutes later a large platter of bacon and scrambled eggs was placed on the mess table by a pasty faced young cook who looked distinctly upset by this change in his nightly routine.

The Australian said: "OK mate, now go back and bring a couple of loaves of bread, a pound of butter and a pot of marmalade. While you are there, start to make a gallon of tea; that's what your big NAAFI teapots hold. Chop, chop."

With these words, he laid the fire axe meaningfully on the table. A lesser man would have backed down in the face of the manager's hostility, but the Australian wasn't looking for a career in Edinburgh or the UK. I hope he found the hospital managers more sympathetic in Australia, but somehow I doubt whether these leopards ever change their spots. As for me, I was glad to go home to my warm little wife just in time for Hogmanay.

Holding hands because the ground was so slippery, we walked from our home in the Dean Village along the Water of Leith into Stockbridge for a New Year party. The world was frozen into a white Arctic silence. The trees along the riverside were draped in frost and icicles as though the City council, in an act of reckless profligacy had ordered the lavish glass and tinsel decoration. Brilliant stars shone from a black velvet sky. We thought of the words of the carol 'Silent Night, Holy Night' and were glad to be alive.

Final Year at Last

The final year kicked off with a series of lectures in psychiatry, picking up where our much earlier introductory lectures had left us five years previously. Psychiatry and I were old friends from the sleep experiment days and as such had no illusions left about each other. This was the first discipline in our final examination; it took place in February, three months ahead of the big stuff. My main lingering impression is of the practical clinical part of the examination in psychiatry.

I spent an hour talking with a man, a hospital inmate, who seemed pretty normal and who had a daytime job in an Edinburgh printing factory. I had been tipped off that all these patients were heavy smokers, so I put a twenty pack of good cigarettes on the table as we opened our discussion. Yes, he had said to the doctors that he heard voices and that he saw visions, but that was because he thought it pleased them. The doctors were friendly to him and he felt very comfortable as a working printer while resident in the hospital. He just wanted to keep this friendly relationship intact.

We talked and talked, but as the bell rang for the last five minutes, I had to say to him that I found his case difficult to diagnose. He said as he pocketed my whole packet of 'Senior Service': "Look, Doc, you've been very generous with your ciggies, so I'll tell you the diagnosis: it's 'Thomson's Leap'."

"Thanks a million," I said as the examining psychiatrist impatiently opened the door of the interview room.

"Well. What's your diagnosis?"

"Schizophrenia, without any doubt. Bizarre phrases. Hears things that other people can't hear and sees things that other people can't see."

"Yes. It's obvious. What took you so long?"

Chalmers Street Hostel

Soon enough Finals took hold of our life, yet some obsessive busy body insisted on us all, shift by shift, spending fourteen nights sleeping in the Chalmers Hostel, connected by tunnel to the Simpson Maternity Pavilion, so that we medical students could be roused to attend demonstrations at night-time of forceps deliveries. It was a colossal waste of time for everyone concerned. I witnessed just one delivery by Kielland's forceps and missed another that was all over before I could get into my trousers.

One curious memory of the hostel is that of lending a fiver to a fellow student whom I didn't know very well. He forgot to pay back before we left Chalmers Street and he ignored several reminders. More important things occupied my mind just three weeks before finals, but after it was all over we still had three weeks to wait for graduation day. I took advantage of an old academic law in Edinburgh, namely that no student owing a debt may graduate. I took my case to the Dean's office and within the week received a cheque and a request for a signed receipt.

About finals itself, there exists a blur. I can't even remember what my long clinical case was nor anything of the short cases. The child in the paediatric long case seemed superficially normal. This simply could not be so in an important exam.

In a desperate last throw of my melting dice, I took out an inch tape and measured the circumference of the two-year-old's head. There it was. The child was in the early stages of hydrocephalus.

Paediatrics didn't appeal to me: it seemed to have too many frightening bats of Hell circling around the innocents lying in the ruddy sandstone building of the Sick Children's hospital. It didn't help to reflect that I had myself, many long winters ago, been one such innocent struggling with diphtheria. The plain truth was that the prospect of facing a paediatric emergency in the deadly still of the night just scared me. In a cruel twist of fate, I found myself, as a trainee anaesthetist in later life, having to deal with many emergency anaesthetics in the Sick Children's hospital.

Again, as a consultant in Fife, the emergency hours brought children galore for urgent surgery. By that time, the black bats no longer bothered me.

Finals and Graduation

Finals passed. Graduation came and went. My parents came up from the Potteries and duly wet a handkerchief over their first child to graduate. Our branch of the Duncan family seemed to contain many potters, engineers and farmers, but no members of the medical profession, so I too felt happy. At the same time, though, I felt rather like a man who, having swum the English Channel, asks himself what should come next.

Judy supplied the answer without hesitation: a holiday in the Italian lakes so that we could start our family. After three years of waiting, she had to be right. It was time for me to stop being a self-centred schoolboy and try to be a serious husband.

The Golden Clinical Years

A medical degree is worthless until the recipient has registered it with the General Medical Council. Catch-22 dictates that this cannot be done until the applicant has satisfactorily completed two six month House Officer appointments, one in medicine and the other in surgery. There was no way around this, and we all knew it.

My first house job was in a terribly busy War Emergency (WE) hospital, hidden behind the Bangour psychiatric hospital. It was an early lesson in the NHS being run on makeshift, just as my old bottle oven pottery factory had been running a year or two ahead of the demolition men. This showed me how the older NHS hospitals had terrible problems that couldn't even be solved by better funding.

Bangour psychiatric hospital, as opposed to the War Emergency Hospital, which stood immediately behind it, was a splendid example of enlightened Victorian healing and caring. Built as a self-maintaining community, where everybody had a job, either in its farm or in its bakery, or laundry or newspaper or carpentry workshop, it even had its own railway station. The acute medical and surgical WE hospital, by contrast, was a worn out makeshift. It had been thrown together quickly on a sloping site in 1939 in anticipation of terrible civilian casualties resulting from the Luftwaffe's bombing our cities.

It was an unattractive group of Nissen huts, makeshift structures intended only for temporary wartime action, but destined to remain in use for forty years. I worked very hard because there was no alternative and because my years as a pottery manager had imbued me with the belief that the best experience of a trade is to be found on the shop floor, or in Bangour's case, on the floor of the ward.

Confident in my industrial experience that overtime earns extra money and that hard work earns hard cash, I felt a warm glow in anticipation of my first payslip. Having worked an average of one hundred hours per week for a month, with many of these hours being during the night, even on the lowest industrial rate, I should have been due over a hundred pounds. My pay cheque at the end of October was for thirty-two pounds. Eight pounds a week for working my newly qualified butt end off! Even street sweepers were better paid!

I marched off to confront the hospital manager/secretary, who was very soothing and soft soapy, but they had me by forelock and foreskin. If I stormed off, the NHS network would black-list me, so that I could work nowhere in the UK as a house officer. General practice was closed to me until I had done a minimum of two house jobs and registered my qualification with the General Medical Council. The only alternative was to emigrate to Australia and to register with their equivalent of the GMC under the same conditions of two house jobs, probably in the Bush.

I could also have chosen to emigrate to the USA or Canada after passing their examination for foreign medical graduates (the ECFMG). Half a dozen of my classmates had taken that course deliberately, having prepared their landing sites by working there during two or three summer vacations. I, however, was a married man with a pregnant wife and my only option was to bloody well get on with it.

Bangour was a tough job; busy and not rewarding financially, as I have explained. Nor was it rewarding career wise. The patients, though, were almost uniformly pleasant, salt of the earth people, teasing me with bits of the local dialect.

For example, the men, knowing that I'd been up all night, would ask: "When's lowsing time, doc?"

This translated as 'when do you loosen the horse's harness, and knock off?'

It was the opposite of 'Yuckin time', or yoking time, when the day started.

My female patients took my breath away by their thoughtfulness and generosity one winter Saturday. Due to my female co-resident house officer having contracted 'flu, I had been continuously on duty for fifteen days. Two fellow residents, from a different unit, Melvin Dewar and Kumar Latchman, out of the kindness of their hearts, took pity on me and covered my wards over the weekend. The ladies in the ward, knowing that I had a wife in Edinburgh, pressed into my arms a huge bouquet of flowers, culled from the best offerings on their ward. It made up for the remote coolness of the senior staff.

My ward Sister at Bangour also did me several great kindnesses, for example, when, after a particularly heavy night in the ward, she did my early morning bloods round so that I might get a little more sleep. These daily blood samples were a heavy chore and entailed doing sedimentation rates

(ESR) on each sample. It was not unusual to get a mouthful of blood from the sampling pipette, but that was before HIV or Hep B had registered as a likely hazard on the clinical danger scale. This was a practical lesson in basic doctor/nurse relations: only a very stupid House Officer would antagonise the Ward Sister.

The resident junior medical doctor was expected to do routine ECGs on admission, using a simple, one track machine in a heavy wooden box. They were called portable ECGs, so they had to be carried around by a brass handle and their use could be demanded anywhere in the hospital. I have unpleasant memories of the occasion when I was summoned on an uphill trek to theatre (remember, the hospital was built on a slope) to monitor a particularly bloody operation on a child of ten who had been horribly mauled in a road traffic accident. I spent an unforgettably awful hour underneath the operating table.

Blood and disinfectant poured down on my crouched form, completely destroying any pretence at sterile precautions or planned procedure. Monitoring the child's heart rate for the anaesthetist, I became vividly aware of how little equipment those country operating theatres had. They could best be compared to early biplanes, flying without an altimeter or compass. Little did I guess that many years in the future I should spend my career as a sort of Biggles anaesthetist, converting a country operating theatre from the equivalent of a primitive biplane to the equivalent of an Airbus.

At the Bangour WE hospital, emergency medicine simply rolled up at the ward door all the time, so the resident's sleep was constantly interrupted. On one horrific night, I was called to the female ward to find myself dealing with two coronaries at the same time. Just as I was taking out a coin to toss to choose which one to do first, a nurse came streaking in from the male ward with the news that Mr X was vomiting bright red blood. Number three, therefore, had to come first.

By the time, I got back to the female ward, one of the emergency admissions was dead, so I just had one to examine and treat. It is possible that both would have done better to stay in bed at home, rather than rattle around in a cold ambulance before getting into a cold, hard hospital bed in a cold, dark, unfamiliar ward where there was no friendly hand to hold.

Nobody asked why I had not called for back-up because nobody wanted to admit that there was none. Both my Senior Registrar and Consultant lived fifteen miles away in Edinburgh and regarded themselves as exempt from night work on account of age. There was no other doctor to call upon. It was called a good experience, but it felt like slave labour. Being constantly 'on call' for a fortnight at Bangour WE hospital was somewhat akin to the Great Sleep Deprivation experiment.

Leaving Bangour WE hospital without regret, it was seriously debatable whether medicine was appropriate for me. It was saddening and depressing that the medical profession should allow its junior members to accept working conditions right out of the Poor Law rule book. A single man, perhaps, would have made yet another career change. I was not a single man: I was a serious husband with a pregnant wife and there was no choice but to soldier on.

Bangour WE was a worn out vestige of its original self with a weary consultant staff who were constantly hoping for a new hospital, so many times promised and so long deferred. They knew that the Regional hospital board regarded them as a low priority and they knew that major refurbishment was being delayed on the pretext of providing a new hospital. They had to wait nearly twenty more years for work to begin on their new hospital at Livingstone.

The Edinburgh Royal Infirmary

I moved into the Royal Infirmary the morning after leaving Bangour. The next six years moulded my medical attitudes and training.

It was with a feeling of joyful liberation that I pushed open the tall glass doors of Ward Ten. Uppermost in my mind was the thought that I had moved from being a mere galley slave rowing a leaky old tub that was long past its most extreme expiry date, to being a privileged member of the Wardroom of a mighty flagship. It struck me immediately on entering that morale in the ERI was high, that far from grumbling at their heavy workload, the whole junior staff delighted in their ability to take on the most difficult tasks.

Partly, this was attributable to the in-depth back-up from consultant and specialist staff. Esprit de Corps started at the top. Every surgeon, every physician and every nurse was proud to be part of the Edinburgh Royal Infirmary. The junior was always able to call for advice or practical help and was expected to do so rather than put any patient at risk of harm. The other contributing factor was that the senior staff for the entire city of Edinburgh had combined to organise work rosters that were sensible and sustainable.

A rota for emergencies was worked out weeks in advance, covering the hospitals of the whole city of Edinburgh. Emergencies in Surgery and Medicine were systematically divided among the various hospital units in 'Waiting Days', which literally meant being on take for twenty-four hours at a time. There was order, predictability and dependability in this hospital. Above all, the young doctor, could develop a feeling of security and still know that his small contribution counted.

The Residents' Mess at Edinburgh Royal Infirmary

To enter the Mess at the Royal Infirmary was to enter a sort of P. G. Woodhouse club: an unreal, even artificial world, but very likeable. The pantomime fat boy, the Mess Butler, clad in a black waistcoat and black bow tie, certainly entered readily into his role as Jeeves, the worldly wise butler. With exaggerated courtesy, he ushered the fresh arrivals to their bedroom and showed off the facilities of this two floor, stone built building. It had two main doors: one from the small car park for the Mess, right opposite the hospital superintendent's house, and the other connecting with a major hospital corridor, halfway between the Medical block and the Surgical block.

Both doors were prominently labelled 'RESIDENCY. Doctors Only'. On entering the Mess from the body of the hospital, we were almost immediately confronted by two long rows of coat hooks, some bearing white coats. These coat hooks flanked the doorway into a large, well-lit dining room where, three times a day, between forty and fifty young doctors took breakfast, lunch and dinner. This was the butler's sovereign territory, where he tried to live in a fantasy written by P. G. Wodehouse. In vain he exerted his tiny authority over the unruly.

As we passed the coat hooks, he turned, his smiling Empress of Blandings piggy face abristle with white stubble and said to us: "The young gentlemen never come to table in their white coat. The Mess Treasurer will impose a fine of one pound on any transgressor and they have their ways of getting the money."

The Mess butler then drew us into the large dining room, a place rather simply furnished with one very large table and one somewhat smaller. Hanging on the walls around this room were some dozen tabletops that had clearly served the Mess at some time. They were heavily carved with the names or initials of former resident members of the Mess, some boards going back into the last century. One more recent board, to which the butler drew our attention, displayed in large letters the name: 'Philip'.

"I remember that evening very well. The Duke was guest of honour at Mess Night and he made a speech. I don't remember what he said but it made the young gentlemen laugh."

He pointed out the warming cupboards in his butler's pantry, saying: "There is always a cold supper left on the small table for when the doctors are working late and these warm shelves sometimes have food on them from when a doctor gets called away in the middle of his meal."

The butler seemed quite blind to the fact that at least ten of his 'young Gentlemen' were very attractive young women and that there had been a 'Ladies Bathroom' in the Mess for thirty years or so. That was not entirely out of character for a

Jeeves, whose life in the Wodehouse novels was repeatedly complicated by the machinations of very domineering young women. He was caught up in a fantasy world where he was the comic butler and where things never changed.

In his Wodehouse world, with his double chins wobbling and lugubrious as a paid mourner at an Irish funeral, our butler, like his 'young gentlemen', was dedicated to the continuation of a tradition. He knew from long experience of 'the young gentlemen' that he could fill the breakfast table in ten minutes simply by opening the inner door between the pantry and the bedroom corridors. There is something particularly stimulating, invigorating, even life affirming about the smell of fresh coffee and frying bacon in the early morning. Generations of guest house owners have known for years that the youthful British male can be summoned from the deepest slumber to appear at the breakfast table in much less time than it takes to dry behind the ears simply by allowing these sweet aromas to drift into the house.

Our tour of the Residence included a large upstairs sitting room for entertaining visitors and where young doctors danced on Saturday evenings to gramophone records played on an elderly PYE radiogram. As he was a bachelor, our Senior Registrar, Iain McLaren, often showed up at these evenings; it had something to do with a tall blonde resident, whom he later married. There was a large billiards table in a lonely upstairs room and the inevitable TV room downstairs.

The bedrooms in the Residence were rather Spartan, with linoleum flooring, relieved only by a small patch of carpet at the bedside. Each room contained a washbasin with plenty of hot water constantly available, as might have been expected in a building whose boilers could have powered the RMS

'Queen Mary'. The bed itself was, of course, a hospital ward bed, tall, hard and cold.

Beside it was placed the inevitable, inescapable black telephone on which we could answer urgent 'bleeps' on our paging device, that invisible chain binding us to our duty. We were not expected to make much use of room or bed, and I forget just how much we were charged for bed and board, but, to my wife's delight, it did include laundry and dry cleaning, so I could always have a clean shirt.

On that first day in Wards 9 & 10, Iain McLaren had arranged everything for a smooth transition from one set of house officers to the next and gave us the afternoon off until 5:30. Ross Barnetson and I played tennis on the hospital asphalt courts, just outside the nurses home called 'The Flo' (for Florence Nightingale). Despite our having been classmates for three years, Ross and I scarcely knew each other; there was a big gap in ages and in background. He was in public school; I was in grammar school.

Ross took the initiative: "Look, this situation is awkward for both of us. This job could be a disaster or we could just agree to damn well make it work. Forget about our attitudes in the final year; let's just make it a success. I married our classmate, Ann Corson, two days after graduation.

She and I already share a bedroom here in the Mess, so I'll take the first night on call. It won't be heavy because the Western is on take for surgical emergencies. Let's go and have a drink at Sandy Bell's. We won't get another chance for six months."

How could anyone fail to get along with such a common sense co-resident?

Iain 'Flash' McLaren was our new Senior Registrar and he is mentioned before our consultants because the Senior Registrars literally ran the Royal Infirmary (with a lot of help from the Ward Sisters) Short, lean and with shiny black hair, McLaren was really our day to day boss and a very good model to follow. He had only just returned to full duty after a thoracotomy, and perhaps, as a result, spoke with a deeply resonant voice. He may have been a slow enough surgeon to earn the title 'Flash', but he was meticulous and neat; accordingly, his operative patients generally did well. Ian McLaren became my role model, not only in surgery but also in his kindly and humane attitude to his patients.

Our consultants were 'Jolly' Jim Jeffrey and Ian Sinclair, both accomplished surgeons and both civil to their junior staff in a somewhat distant way. Early in our residents' job, Sinclair demonstrated to us that he was more than just a pretty face when he hauled from death's grasp a moribund young airman. This eighteen-year-old man/boy had undergone a 'routine' appendicectomy the previous week, but, instead of bouncing back to parade ground fitness, his health had perversely deteriorated.

An abscess of the appendix stump was assumed, but there was nothing to be seen. It was early evening. Sinclair was called in to sort out this abnormal peritonitis. He gave a master class on abdominal surgery, starting from the dictum: "Pus somewhere; pus nowhere means pus under the diaphragm."

He put both arms up to the elbow round the boy's liver and swept his hands under the diaphragm and over the liver. Smelly yellow pus-filled the abdominal cavity and Sinclair retired for five minutes to change his gloves and gown before washing out the mess. This time the airman made a rapid recovery, while two House Surgeons had learned something valuable.

James Sneddon Jeffrey was a complex character whose wartime career was certainly brilliant. It was no small achievement to start the war as a captain in the Edinburgh Territorial Army Field Hospital and to finish it as a brigadier. At the war's end, it took time for men like J. S. Jeffrey to work their way into consultant posts in the Royal Infirmary and had their return not coincided with the foundation of the NHS and the rapid expansion of hospital services, many might have been forced to pursue their career abroad.

The same bitterness that I had noticed in the ex-servicemen returning to the pottery factories was to be found in the consultant ranks in ERI. Not surprisingly, a certain dourness of expression in Mr Jeffrey had led his juniors to dub him 'Jolly Jim', though never to his grim face.

Little by little, from tiny bits and scraps of conversation overheard or passed on, it was possible to build up a fuller picture of Jolly Jim. Most of this came from Iain McLaren, who often assisted him in theatre and who actually managed the daily running of the Wards. Jolly Jim operated in stony silence and detested any intrusion while engaged in operating. The same was also true for most of the war surgeons, possibly because they still felt the pressures of battle piling more and more desperately wounded and bleeding casualties at their door.

Iain McLaren was quite the opposite. Even though he had been at war in Suez for eight days, Iain produced a non-stop monologue while meticulously, neatly, carefully working his way through an operating list, even at 2 o'clock in the morning.

It was an interruption one morning, while Jolly Jim was operating that gave the first clue that a deeply suppressed sense of mischief and humour lay waiting inside him. The medical superintendent of ERI, in full tweeds and country brogues, barged into the sterile surroundings of the theatre while Jim, who still called himself a general surgeon, was amputating a leg. Like all doctors, he regarded the management to be in league with the Devil and here was one pretending that rules of cleanliness and sterility did not apply to him.

Whether by chance or by design, Jolly Jim released an arterial clamp just as this man stamped up the six terrazzo steps from the showers to the theatre. The jet of blood shot eight feet across the room and hit the wall just inches short of the intruder. An alarmed and possibly chastened manager quickly withdrew, saying something into his handkerchief.

It has already been mentioned that the Senior Registrars managed the daily business of the wards and did nearly all the emergency surgery. These men (and in the 1960s, there were no female surgical Senior Registrars in the Royal) were almost all in their thirties. It was usual for them to be nearly forty before receiving a consultant appointment. This being so, they were, in effect, surgeons of great experience and considered it a weakness to be obliged to call in their consultant, especially after bedtime.

It was, therefore, a serious moment when one night, in the middle of dealing with an emergency, Iain McLaren laid down his knife and decided to call in Jolly Jim. He knew that this might spoil his chances of getting the latter's full support when the next consultant post came along, but he felt that, with this particular case, he was out of his depth. Although the patient was a thorough villain, a brothel protector and a thug, Iain still refused to take chances with human life.

Jolly Jim came in and was not at all amused at the story of two brothel protectors, fighting a knife duel with two other thugs eager to take over their 'duties'. What at first glance was a trivial neck wound, no more than an inch long, turned out to be a traditional assassin's blow, usually delivered with a long poniard or commando knife. After an hour's fruitless messing around and with endless blood loss, Jim, in his turn, laid down his knife and decided to call in the thoracic surgeon.

Ben LaRue, who later became Professor of Cardiac surgery in Cape Town, took over. J. S. Jeffrey became his assistant, with Iain McLaren as the second assistant. Meanwhile, I had to return to the ward to examine the other brother, who, like a true 'hard man' was trying to kid the police that he was perfectly all right, despite four puncture wounds in his back.

The detective constable in charge of him was bitingly open in his contempt, deeply regretting a lifetime committed to involvement with such 'crud'. Theatre finished at 4:00 in the morning and Big Harry was moved upstairs to the care of the cardiothoracic surgeons. I counted the used polythene bags of blood; there were thirty-two.

After four hours of rest, I reported back to the ward to find Jolly Jim looking fresh and pleasant. The night's work had clearly brought back old memories and at the same time secured a good recommendation for his senior registrar. As House Officer, I was sent up to the Thoracic surgeons on a goodwill visit. They had put their seriously ill knife wound patient into a side room, guarded by a policeman who sat on a hard chair beside the door.

Once inside the room, the CT house officer listed the patient's surgery as though I had never had sight nor smell of him. The knife wound in his neck had penetrated deeply, severing most of the nerves and arteries of the left arm; this had accordingly been removed as irreparable. The knife had sliced open several inches of the oesophagus and ascending aorta. All this could only be properly viewed by splitting the sternum to open the rib cage. Heavily wrapped in bandages, this mess of a man looked no danger to anybody.

Mr LaRue's Ward Sister was fussing around this wreck, arranging some flowers and showing him his mail. As early as this, some cards were arriving. It was amazing how quickly news spread. Even as we stood there, Sister held up a large envelope and opened it for her one-armed patient. Inside was a black-edged card, bearing the handwritten greeting: "We'll get you soon, Harry."

Harry committed suicide a few days later by drinking a pint of cigarette lighter fuel. He died in the agonies of liver and kidney failure.

Jolly Jim enjoyed being Chief and the minor ceremonials that went with that honour, foremost among which was the fuss of being shepherded to the main door of ERI by his clinical staff. A collection of white coats flapped after him at 12:45, like a flock of geese after the mother bird. It was, therefore, a considerable annoyance to him when one bright morning in summer, his clinical secretary stopped him at the ward door with a sheaf of papers, which she suggested, demanded his immediate attention.

"You have to draw up your list of candidates for your next SHO appointment."

"Oh, that can wait until tomorrow."

"The University Secretary's office says that we must reply today or vacate the post."

"Oh, bother! How many names are there?"

"Twenty-four, Mr Jeffrey."

"Take off the foreign names. How many are left?"

"Twelve, Sir."

"How many Scots names have we?"

"Six, Sir."

"Send them all for interview. Now if that is all, I am off for lunch. I am called to the country this afternoon. McLaren, you have my phone number in case of need."

An assured and happy man, Jolly Jim strode off to the front door, down the long corridor, its black and white floor tiles shining and smiling respectfully. His white-clad attendants flapped along after him like so many geese behind mother goose. Then, upon the departure of the chief and the boom of the 1 o'clock gun from the castle, they took off like startled birds to head for lunch in the Mess.

The Visit of the Lord High Commissioner

The same scene was repeated, but in reverse when, a few weeks later, wards 9 & 10 were given the honour of hosting the annual visit of the Lord High Commissioner. This office results from the Queen being simultaneously head of two separate churches. She cannot, as the anointed head of the Church of England, attend the annual General Assembly of the Church of Scotland without resolving this conflict of loyalties, so a deputy is appointed in her place, hence the Lord High Commissioner.

With great ceremony, this very important person arrived at the consultants' car park. An elderly black limousine, one of the Queen's Rolls-Royces, deposited on the steps of the massive front door, a tall kilted man, the feathers in his bonnet, proclaiming that he belonged to the Honourable Company of Archers, the Queen's official bodyguard in Scotland. Before him stood a small group of senior figures: the hospital manager, the accountant, the Matron and Jolly Jim. A brief formal greeting on the steps was swiftly followed by another in the main hallway of the Infirmary, where administrative staff were gathered to bob and bow.

White of hair and white of coat, looking the very image of a distinguished surgeon in a Hollywood film, J. S. Jeffrey ushered his important visitor to the door of ward 10, where stood Sister in her best blue uniform with lace collar and white gloves. She was flanked by her three Staff Nurses and a dozen ward nurses. The junior medical staff stood a little further into the ward.

A great deal of preparation had been done for this visit. The nurses had been schooled to courtesy; fresh white aprons and white bonnets had been issued just one hour before the visit. The young doctors had been briefed on clothing: black shoes, well shined; dark trousers, sober tie, white shirt and no jacket to be worn beneath a spotless white coat (specially issued). Iain McLaren and Jolly Jim had carefully picked which patients were to be introduced and which, mainly the very ill, were to be shielded from the excitement by placing them in the six bedded side ward.

In the latter group, Iain McLaren wanted to include a certain Mr X: "Mr X was sentenced to six years for burglary by the present Lord High Commissioner. He might remember Mr X's face."

The notion appealed to Jolly Jim that a High Court judge and law Lord could be induced to shake the hand of an old lag that he had himself sentenced. He turned down his Registrar's suggestion with the words: "Oh, we will call him Mr X, the bus conductor, in case his face rings a bell!"

Jim then turned to Ross and me with an additional bit of advice: "I want you to be at my elbow as we go round the ward; Duncan in Ward 10, Barnetson in Ward 9. Each patient just quietly give me name and occupation. I don't want any medical jargon or diagnosis, just two facts. Neither of you may speak to the Commissioner unless he speaks to you first. You will show him the same respect that you would show Her Majesty."

We, two housemen, were left to wonder how Mr Jeffrey could reconcile his little joke with the need to show respect. Ross suggested that this was an example of one part of the upper circle of Edinburgh society talking on equal terms to its neighbour. Clearly, there was more to Jolly Jim than appeared on the surface.

The Lord High Commissioner cruised sedately round the two wards like a battleship doing a peacetime courtesy visit to a Commonwealth country. His accompanying wife clutching the usual bouquet of flowers, tagged along behind.

The whole affair lasted sixty minutes. The important couple climbed into the elderly limousine and the visit was concluded with ceremonial waving and camera smiles.

Iain McLaren, always a stickler for etiquette, put his head round the door of the Doctors' Room and said: "I'm just going to congratulate Sister on a successful visit. She will be feeling pleased and will be entertaining the nurses to a special tea in her own room. You lot give her an hour to relax and I'll meet you here for the evening ward round at 4:30."

One of the many good things about a resident house officer's life in the Royal Infirmary of Edinburgh was its predictability. Routine is often pooh-poohed as boring, but it can also be comforting to know what is expected and when.

One surgeon, famous for his caustic tongue, put it this way: "You will find that assisting me in theatre is easy. I always do the same things in the same way with the same instruments. You always know what is coming next. God alone can help the surgeon who himself does not know what to do next."

Waiting Night

There were four main operating mornings each week: three for the consultants and one for the Senior Registrar. Inserted into this framework was Waiting Day when the Ward took all general surgical emergencies from the whole of the city. It was a matter of pride among the house officers that they would never turn away an emergency, even when the ward was officially full. Beds could be squeezed more tightly together and then extra beds placed down the middle of the ward and even out into the classroom, dressing room and inner corridor.

It was easy to spot which ward was the Waiting Ward because the porters would stack four disassembled hospital beds at its door in the public corridor. Extra beds were regularly needed, but if by some freak of chance the Waiting Ward admitted no patients, the Ward Sister was entitled to receive the gift of a pair of white gloves from the Senior Registrar on duty.

Waiting Night was when we really brushed and combed our surgical diagnostic skills and when we House officers would occasionally ourselves perform an appendicectomy under the watchful eye of Iain McLaren. The routine for admissions was that the houseman on take would receive a phone call from the GP making the initial diagnosis and giving the salient points about the patient's medical history. As this house officer could not refuse the patient, this call was simply a courtesy, though it could provide very useful background information. The GP could, alternatively, refer the admission to the Bed Bureau.

This bureau was organised by Lothian Health Board and linked up the ambulance service, the hospitals and the GPs. This central control point knew exactly what was the bed state in every ward in every hospital because this information was passed to it every twelve hours by the management. It knew where the ambulances were and how many were available and, most important of all, it knew which wards were on call and when. House officers may have hated the early morning volley of bells squirted into their sleepy ears by the bedside telephone, but there was no denying that the Bed Bureau was an essential tool in the efficient use of hospital beds.

Waiting Day was also an active time for the senior administrative nurses in Matron's office. In ten years at the Royal Infirmary, I never once met the Matron. I knew her name and what she looked like. Matron was a figure much more remote than our surgical consultants, and like them, she preserved certain hauteur, her headgear deliberately staking out her separateness.

Assistant Matrons, mature ladies, of whom there seemed to be several, ran the Royal Infirmary at night. In the role of Night Sister (in those days senior nurses were all female), it was they who would come to the aid of the overworked nurses on a busy Waiting ward. They could also be a source of helpful advice to the junior doctor struggling to reach a decision: they had been there, seen it all before. Night Sister would shunt nurses around from silent, sleeping wards to those in the war zone of frenetic, almost demonic activity.

In case anybody talks to you about bringing back Matron, you should gently chide them that they have been watching too many 'Carry On' films. The Sisters of the Royal Infirmary, together with the Senior Registrars, ran the place. They were the lifeblood, the living muscle and the caring soul without which it would merely have been yet another stone building on the edge of parkland.

Traditionally, the Ward Sister with her nurses cared for a group of patients in a house specially devoted to the nursing of the sick. This arrangement had roots in Medieval times. The more recent Nightingale arrangement was that a doctor would be available to be consulted by the Sister in charge. He would assign to his assistant physicians the daily duties, such as wound dressing and charting progress.

Thus, we have the junior House Officer and his consulting senior colleague both present at the invitation of the ward Sister. Things have changed since 1965, either by evolution or by decree and the old concept of a team of nurses and doctors focused on the care of a group of patients seems to have disappeared. The idea of doctors and nurses working in competition or independently of each other is a recipe for the sort of chaos in-hospital care that so frequently hits the front page of the popular press.

Years after leaving the Royal Infirmary, I asked Ward Sister Ross why she had not joined managerial nursing. She answered that to be a ward sister in ERI was the pinnacle of any nursing career. Management, in her eyes, was for the totally untalented nurse.

Sister Ross, as a devout Catholic, set her standards of care very high and, looking back, it seems probable that she felt called to a life of nursing from religious as well as clinical motives. She was at her happiest when tutoring the occasional squad of novice nursing nuns in training, those good ladies who, at moments of crisis, tended to think in terms of prayer rather than in terms of intravenous drips.

Iain McLaren relished Waiting Day: it was his opportunity to shine and to demonstrate to Jolly Jim that he was indeed ready to take on the heavy responsibilities of a consultant. He had all the necessary qualifications for a consultant in the ERI: he had attended an Edinburgh boys private school and qualified in Edinburgh. He was a Fellow of both the Edinburgh and London Royal College of Surgeons. He had spent a year gaining the BTA (Been To America) by working at a hospital in the USA.

He had seen active military service (a week in Suez). He lacked only a wife, and for this several remedies were available. Iain seemed to be the contented bachelor for whom only his work was serious. He endowed Waiting Night with a ritual that he felt suited his mighty predecessors in Edinburgh surgery, while, at the same time, giving his patients the consideration and care that was their due.

The ritual or routine of Waiting Day was to take red hot emergencies to theatre as soon as possible. These would be anaesthetised by the consultant anaesthetist attached to Wards 9 & 10, a tall, gaunt survivor of military service whose fair hair had become white without altering his smiling appearance. Like so many consultant anaesthetists, he was a silent witness at the operating table, allowing the surgeon to do all the talking or to work in silence if that was preferred.

On Waiting Night, his duties ended at 10:00. Iain McLaren, therefore, tried to schedule all emergencies that would wait until eleven, by which time there would be several hours of operating listed.

McLaren's routine allowed time for the house officers properly to prepare the patients gathered in the ward awaiting emergency surgery but also, in the gap between ten and eleven, for the Waiting Night anaesthetist to examine them and to prescribe premedication. As Senior Registrar, McLaren was in charge of Waiting Day. The junior staff were at his disposal and at his discretion, the SHO and Registrar would be deployed to the theatre to operate, under his supervision, on less difficult cases. All patients admitted to the ward for observation or surgery were there because he had examined them and agreed on the provisional diagnosis.

McLaren knew exactly what was going on and generally was able to take a break between 8:00 pm and 10:00 pm. This became his trademark: a 'man about town' hearty meal at a good restaurant before operating; a bit unusual, maybe even exhibitionist, but indubitably individual. To this ritual meal, he would invite the SHO or Registrar, depending on the delicacy of the balance of probability of trouble in the ward. Sometimes, we would be obliged to ring through to

'Cosmo's' or 'The Cafe Royal' to summon him back to deal with a difficult problem, but this he regarded as an unlucky roll of the dice.

The Gelded Man

There were occasions when Iain McLaren's bachelor habit of a late heavy meal did not quite work out well. On one memorable Waiting Night, a call from A & E came through to the theatre at around two am, summoning the waiting surgeon to take an emergency who was 'Just pissing blood everywhere'. Iain sent me off to look at what sounded like a bladder or kidney problem.

On entering the swing doors of A & E, the first thing to be seen was a figure in a police uniform lying in a large pool of blood. Increasing the horror, this PC rolled over and added the contents of his stomach to the puddle of blood.

The Casualty officer, Al Harvey, called me over to a screened off cubicle, immediately adjacent to this shambles. The scene thereby immediately dissolved into one of comic horror. On a gurney lay a young man with a blood-soaked white towel being compressed between his legs by a red-faced staff nurse. This was our emergency patient.

"Over here, John," shouted our Al.

"The copper's OK. He's the one who brought this guy on the trolley to A & E. He was OK, that is, until I took the towel away to examine the wound and this guy's dick fell onto the floor.

"This customer cut his dick off earlier on.

"Said it was lowering his spiritual centre of gravity.

"Put it on the family Bible and took a cut-throat razor to it.

"Felt elated for a while, then thought the bleeding was upsetting him and went down to the police box at the end of the street.

"He's cross-matched for four and four. Drip's good. Take him away; he's all yours."

As my little trolley party of nurse, theatre orderly and the patient was preparing to set off for Ward 10, two very large policemen came into A & E from the police box at the gates of the Royal Infirmary. They hauled their bloodstained pale colleague onto a vacant gurney with words of sympathy and encouragement: "Bloody fairy! Where do they get guys like you?"

The castrated man was quickly anaesthetised and McLaren set about the repair of the bleeding stump of the penis. He talked with the fond memory of a similar wound that he had treated due to shrapnel injury. He talked about being a country vet and how this would be a normal part of his life, gelding young stallions. He talked about shoes and ships and sealing wax until he suddenly fell silent.

We looked at him standing with a long straight needle inserted at the edge of the stump of the penis but now not moving. Iain McLaren had gone to sleep on his feet. So much for ceremonial meals!

Jolly Jim was much amused by this story, suitably tailored. Still smiling, he said to McLaren: "This fellow is insane and is bound to be troublesome. Get him into Ward 3 under lock and key."

A few days later this prediction proved accurate. Ward 3 asked us to come down and advise regarding 'the gelding's' behaviour. He was marching like a guardsman up and down the long Nightingale ward, his imaginary rifle held on his shoulder. It was no use trying to speak to him; it was necessary first to enter into his fantasy.

The voice of a harsh NCO came out of my mouth: "GUARD, guard HALT. Atten-SHUN. Slope arms. Stand at HIZE. Stand easy. Fall out."

Then we could have a little talk about his wound and his general health.

A Sketchy Outline of
Jolly Jim Jeffrey

Life in Wards 9 & 10 was far from dull and perhaps I have written too much about the senior consultant surgeon, J. S. Jeffrey, but he remains for me, not so much a hero but rather a complex and intriguing character who had figured in heroic developments. He did not seek popularity, but his important part in the development of Penicillin antibiotics seems strangely neglected. I admired him. Above all, it was the experience of working in his wards in the ERI that confirmed my choice of medicine as a career. I, therefore, add his name to the list of those whom I must thank.

As a schoolboy at George Watson's School, he developed an interest in the arts and later took an MA at Edinburgh University, which was entirely wrong for a budding surgeon in the days when they were supposed all to be Philistines. (Perhaps he was initially heading for a career in Law.)

At the same time, he was awarded a University 'Blue' for rugby and had a trial for the Scottish International team, which, in turn, was wrong again. The physicians, the intellectuals of the medical profession, scorned the 'muddy oafs' of the playing fields. To even the score, JSJ was an ardent golfer, a lifelong member of the Muirfield club which occasionally hosted The Open.

His joy at winning the College of Surgeons' annual challenge plate in 1965 was obvious and totally unconcealed.

What prompted his taking up the medicine I have no idea, but it may have had something to do with the General Strike of 1926, the year that he graduated MA. In a conversation with Iain McLaren, I heard him recall being one of two student volunteer locomotive drivers/firemen when the engine that they were supposed to be returning to Edinburgh had run out of steam on the Forth Bridge. The two volunteer firemen had allowed the fire to run too low in their efforts to save coal (the miners' strike was at the heart of the dispute) and they had too little left to raise steam again. It was then that they discovered that there is a distinct gradient to the track on the bridge itself and that he and the other student could push their engine to the safety of a siding in Inverkeithing.

Great national upheavals like Brexit, or Suez, or The General Strike quite understandably can cause young people to change careers. Older people, who don't understand or who disapprove often call this 'revolt', but really it is simply a recognition that major upheavals have altered the course of some of life's great rivers.

J. S. Jeffrey qualified in medicine rather later than his contemporaries and, as he obviously had private means, he chose to undergo surgical training in the Royal Infirmary of Edinburgh. In the 1930s, this was rather like trying to learn navigation by rowing as a galley slave. He, nevertheless, found time to complete an MD thesis on Crohn's disease. Both payment and leisure time were ridiculously small and this may have influenced his decision to join the Territorial

Army, Edinburgh Field Hospital Unit, which entitled him to paid annual leave and a small extra salary. This choice resulted in his rapid dispatch to France in September 1939.

In the winter of 1939/1940, Major Jeffrey had written an article on 'The use of Sulphonamide powder in the treatment of wounds' and it had been published in *The British Medical Journal*. This article may have prompted the military authorities in 1942 to select the Major to conduct the clinical trials in Egypt of a new anti-bacterial called Penicillin.

Professor Florey had brought out to Egypt a leather suitcase containing the world's entire supply of this test drug in the form of large ampoules of a cloudy liquid. The conversation, terse and military, probably went something like this: "There is no time for animal trials. Anyway, the only trial that matters is on human beings. We know nothing about this stuff except that it wipes out Gram-positive bacteria in the laboratory. It may be absolute bloody poison, so only use it on the most seriously wounded that are likely to develop gangrene or tetanus; those who are probably doomed to die already."

JSJ: "What sort of dosage do you recommend?"

"The writing on the ampoules tells you that they each contain a million units of Penicillin. That is a laboratory measurement and means nothing, as yet, in clinical use. Each ampoule contains one thousand millilitres, so that's ten thousand units per ten ml. Call that one hundred doses and give three doses a day by intramuscular injection."

JSJ examined all sixty men in a smelly acute ward, taking full clinical notes. He instructed the army nurses in the dosage and timing of injections and went away for forty-eight hours. Using what today would be regarded as ridiculously

171

inadequate doses, a miracle had been wrought in this short time. Men who had been dying only forty-eight hours ago were now sitting up in bed and shouting for breakfast.

Despite recycling penicillin from the treated patients' urine, supplies ran out after six weeks. Major now Colonel Jeffrey wrote his report. The war continued and wounds still became gangrenous, but penicillin remained a laboratory product made by hand in pitifully inadequate amounts.

It was because the need was so urgent and because British pharmaceutical companies lacked the resources that the British Government sought the expertise of the huge pharmaceutical giants in the USA to mass-produce this miracle drug. There had, over the preceding two years, already been some research work done on Penicillin in New York's Columbia University laboratories. Because there were so many and varied strains of Penicillin moulds and because Fleming had not precisely identified his original mould strain, the Oxford group had sent out to research groups in North America a request for Penicillin cultures. Columbia Presbyterian Medical Centre had received a Rockefeller research grant and had established a connection with Florey's group in Oxford. They had, indeed, produced and tried on patients a form of medicinal penicillin.

Patent Rights

At this point in the story of Penicillin, a matter arose of great concern: patent rights. The US Government had funded the research into the mass production of Penicillin and refused to allow any US patent rights to a drug that had been produced by pubic money. The British research workers similarly refused to take out patent rights because they also felt that the public should have the benefit of the research that had been publicly funded.

The patent rights to Penicillin were a matter of vital concern to the US pharmaceutical industry. Understandably, big corporations were reluctant to invest the huge sums necessary to mass-produce Penicillin without first securing the assurance of a profitable return. The great contribution to the drug's production on a large scale had come from laboratories of the US Department of Agriculture in Peoria, Illinois. There, a process of fermentation using corn steep liquor had increased penicillin production by tenfold. It was fitting, therefore, that the process of industrial manufacture should be granted the patent rather than the antibiotic itself.

Considerations of profit, patent rights and ownership of penicillin became irrelevant. The world had gained its first antibiotic and millions of lives have since been saved by it.

James S. Jeffrey returned to Edinburgh at the end of the war as a Brigadier and became the Royal Infirmary's expert on the treatment of Tetanus. He returned to the Edinburgh surgical scene just as many other doctors were returning from military service, some with senior rank, some harrowed to their core by terrible experiences, some dripping with medals and decorations, but mostly just happy to return to normal life.

In the corridors of the Royal Infirmary, the students would pass a Professor of surgery who had been Brigadier in charge of surgical services to the British Army in Burma, and his anaesthetist who had been an MO at the siege of Kohima. In this place, one might meet a physician who had helped to pioneer scuba diving frogmen, a psychiatrist who had devised interrogation techniques, a physiologist who had supervised

173

the treatment of starving POWs released from Japanese concentration camps, a professor of Orthopaedic surgery who had been dropped by parachute into the guerrilla mountains of Yugoslavia, and many others with a fascinating background story. Like so many, JSJ had done his whack in the period 1939–1945 and that the rest of his career should have been a gentle cruise, avoiding all further rocks and shipwrecks. That he was not elected President of the Royal College of Surgeons in Edinburgh must, I feel, have been due to personal factors.

Jolly Jim had a sense of humour that allowed him to join in a joke. For example, I got a bit carried away just two days before the end of my house job in Wards 9 & 10. It was JJ's operating day and it was also his birthday, so I very cheekily painted in skin cleansing solution on the belly of his unconscious patient in the anaesthetic room, the message: "Happy Birthday, Jim."

In his office, trying to explain my behaviour. I could only apologise and say that the experience of working as his house officer had been so enjoyable that it had altered my view of a career in medicine. I had allowed myself to get carried away, maybe, but it was true. It had been a great experience to be a trusted and valued member of his surgical team and now to be looking forward to entering my qualification on the Medical Register.

I should have added that all this was very much due to the kindly care and behaviour of his Senior Registrar, Iain McLaren. We shook hands and next met five years later at Jolly Jim's retirement party.

The Questioning or Auditing Tradition of the Eri

It was a practical truism in the Edinburgh Royal Infirmary that we all can learn from our own mistakes and from the mistakes of others. This was in the days before it could be labelled 'Clinical Audit', but that's exactly what it was. Without any whistle-blowers or penalty points, the search for the truth plodded forward modestly. Without any blowing of trumpets or rattling of chains, these meetings achieved results that eluded the later hospital managers, with their childish efforts to avoid accountability.

In this spirit of non-accusatorial inquiry, there was held in the large Surgical Lecture theatre, on the first Saturday of every month, a special meeting, which had acquired the unofficial title of 'The Death Meeting'. The surgical teams took it in turns to present their less successful cases, or disasters. These meetings were supposed to be for auditing and learning purposes. Behind locked doors, the truth could be revealed and criticisms made which would never be made public. There was to be no such thing as a cover-up, for 'reason ends where mystery begins'.

On other Saturdays, the consultants and senior registrars would present short case studies or papers on their own research projects, but showing off or being a clever-clever was absolutely not done at Death Meetings: they were about learning, not about scoring points and definitely not about attributing blame.

Being a junior doctor was very similar to my industrial apprenticeship in Stoke. We were there to look and learn, to do the chores, to work under supervision and to keep our patients safe. Very early in my apprenticeship in ERI, a situation arose that emphasised our need to learn, no matter how senior we were. It was a clear illustration of the limitations of even a well-handled audit.

The cardiothoracic surgeons had been humiliated by their high post-operative death rate due to chest infections among their patients undergoing heart valve replacements. Infection rates among their patients undergoing shorter procedures remained low. Despite elaborate anti-bacterial preparations, including extensive personal washing, shampooing and stuffing anti-bacterial pledgets into the nose; despite discarding every stitch of clothing, including socks, and donning sterile operating clothes; despite the bacterial monitoring of every person in the theatre or attending to the post-operative care of 'pump patients'; despite everything these cardiac patients continued to get massive chest infections and to die from them.

A wide variety of antibiotics was tried and no particular organism seemed to be obviously responsible. It was a baffling situation and it defied two 'death meetings'. In retrospect, the 'invisible gorilla' was sitting in the middle of the audience.

The final explanation was a good example of a large group of highly intelligent people missing the obvious because nobody had challenged the initial objective of the inquiry. From the start, it was assumed that some microorganism lay at the root of these deaths. Backed up by X-rays that showed sometimes disturbingly dense blotches, sometimes widespread small beads, the diagnosis seemed secure.

Nobody had even considered that such X-rays could mean anything other than infection. Nobody could explain why this long series of infections had been totally resistant to antibiotics. Nobody could suggest a causative organism. At last, in a desperate attempt to pin down the identity of this resistant bacterium, fungus or virus, two anaesthetists had gone down to the mortuary room and taken a sample of such lesions under direct vision so that they could be fully scrutinised by the bacteriology laboratory. The answer came back that these masses in the dead lungs were not bacterial at all. The X-rays had been showing deposits of silicone wax, both large and small.

During the four hour operation to replace a heart valve, the heart had to be stopped and oxygenated blood to the brain and body supplied by a by-pass system colloquially called 'the pump'. At the centre of this system was the Rygge bag, a large and complex plastic reservoir that contained several litres of blood, through which oxygen was bubbled. The blood had been stored in a laboratory fridge and needed to be warmed to body temperature in the Rygge bag.

Nobody, least of all the manufacturers, had any idea that the light coating of silicone wax was soluble. It was used to prevent blood from sticking to the plastic walls of the bag, but the heating process had caused it to melt and to enter the lungs of the patient on by-pass. The obvious only became obvious when every other possibility had been discarded.

A year or two later, this spirit of inquiry came to the rescue, not only of myself but of the Department of Anaesthetics and the Royal Infirmary medical staff. After a series of disastrous failures to resuscitate barbiturate overdose patients in A & E, two of the junior anaesthetists were encouraged by their Professor to hold a clinical meeting on the subject of 'cardiac arrest'. Cardiac resuscitation was still in its infancy in 1966, but as a lecture subject, it was already being regarded as yawn-making stuff. The Anaesthetics Department held Wednesday afternoon teaching meetings, just as the Department of Surgery held its Saturday morning sessions, yet the two most junior members of the anaesthetics department were surprised that what we regarded as a cry for help should have attracted so large an audience.

As four of these patients under study were destined for the 'Poisons Unit' under the care of a very distinguished physician we had taken the precaution of asking his permission to view their notes. To our amazement, Dr Henry Matthew, the eponymous consultant turned up with a large staff. After our presentation, there was a general discussion, attempting to clarify why four people should die while breathing pure oxygen.

Dr Matthew, head of the poisons unit summed up his own view: "It could be said that statistically, all four barbiturate overdose patients fall within the five per cent death rate to be expected from such poisoning. Statistics can be misleading, though, and while it would be possible for our statistically acceptable four deaths to occur within six weeks, it would be most unusual and I don't believe it. I simply don't know why these four died."

A few days later, barbiturate overdose number five died under resuscitation in A&E. This death occurred at 11:00 in the morning, unlike the preceding four which had all been after ten at night. Blood gases revealed a total absence of serum oxygen in arterial blood samples taken post-mortem. Direct sampling of the oxygen and nitrous oxide wall points revealed that the oxygen and nitrous oxide pipelines had been crossed over. Once again the obvious answer had been missed.

A total embargo on information relating to these deaths was immediately imposed by the hospital management. Nevertheless, the story was leaked to the daily press. They created an atmosphere of almost hysterical terror in the public mind. Every day the papers leaked a little more information into the public domain, while the hospital management simply fed fuel to the fire of fear by refusing to comment. Eventually, this whole silly facade broke and the police took over the investigations.

A few weeks later, a High Court judge absolved the anaesthetists and medical staff involved from his very severe criticisms of the hospital management and the company whose installers had crossed oxygen and nitrous oxide gas pipes.

He said, in summary: "The medical staff suspected that something was wrong and they with their colleagues made all efforts within their power to identify their problem. That they failed to do so is unfortunate but by no means blameworthy."

This is an example to justify honesty as the best policy. It is also another example of a group of highly intelligent people missing the obvious—i.e. that these people had all died through lack of oxygen. In fact, one Senior Registrar, Bill

Barge, said just that. He was unable to explain how this could have happened when they were all receiving pure oxygen from the newly installed wall pipeline.

We had misled ourselves by adopting as a sure fact that the wall system was an absolutely reliable source of pure oxygen. Had it been installed by the British Oxygen Company, our confidence would have been well-founded. This, alas, was the work of an inexperienced company. They had not bothered to check that the gas in the new pipeline really was oxygen, whereas, something that BOC did routinely was to test the quality of its own work.

A Winter Spent in A & E

Popular films, like 'Doctor in the House' and the 'Carry on' series make believe that a doctor's work in the hospital is a light-hearted comedy parade. I would hate to pass on that impression: it is damn hard work and only the most stout-hearted young doctors and nurses survive. Hospitals exist for two purposes: first, to assist the safe delivery of healthy babies and to mend what is broken in body or mind; second, to teach young doctors and nurses the essentials of medicine and surgery. This is a very broad remit and the cynic may say that A & E is where those seeking help are sorted into categories by those seeking experience.

There is a large grain of truth in that, but the system in the ERI was stabilised by the close supervisory role of two experienced consultant surgeons, who would read the 'logbook' of the overnight happenings and discuss with the staff the problems of the day before handing over to two experienced surgical Registrars. The staff doctors had access as of right to the help of all the specialist departments. This sort of close back-up was intended to ensure that junior doctors in A & E did not feel isolated or left to deal with problems that were beyond their capabilities. There was also a plainly stated rule that no surgical registrar, no matter how brilliant, could be appointed to Senior Registrar without first having served a long and thorough apprenticeship, and this included twelve months in A&E. It was clearly indicated that this was no mere dumping ground for the untalented, as it might be in more minor hospitals.

Here we encounter another widely held misapprehension about the NHS and hospitals in general. The NHS, whatever it is now, was not a monolithic administration and hospitals varied widely from one end of the country to the other. Some of the medical profession wrongly believe the oft-repeated dictum that 'every hospital is a teaching hospital'; nothing could be further from the truth. That is why it is important to depict Edinburgh Royal Infirmary in its golden age, to show just how good the best can be.

To say that A & E was always busy is merely to state the b******g obvious. It went full bore from 0830 to 0300. There was often a slack period in the night between 0300 and 0600, hence the presence in the doctors' duty room of a large black leather 'chaise long' on which the white-coated hero could relax. This sleep was of the fitful kind, as the ambulances of the sixties were equipped with long wire radio aerials and the portal of A & E was protected from rain and snow by a large glass awning held up on cast iron brackets.

The wire aerials counted the brackets outside the open window of the doctors' duty room as they rolled slowly up to the front entrance of A & E: 'One boing, Two boing, Three boing, Four boing', serving to awaken the duty casualty officer. Quite often the arriving patient was booked into the care of a physician by telephone and required no examination or attention, so the duty doctor could sleep on undisturbed.

This wee pinch of sleep in the small hours was all the idleness that the night shift could offer. At weekends and at bank holidays the pressure continued throughout the night, with a continued stream of foul-mouthed drunks, with cut heads, broken bones and alcoholic poisonings. The culminating horror was Hogmanay. The disgusting smell of blood and alcohol was a revolting warning that there is nothing funny about a drunk. Edinburgh policemen, who were frequent (and welcome) visitors to A & E, certainly did not find drunks amusing and made sure that the holding cells in the High Street Police Headquarters offered neither comfort nor hospitality.

Relations between police and A & E were cordial on both sides and helped by the presence of a constantly manned police box, just twenty metres from the main door of Casualty. A young doctor, backed up against the white tiled walls by a thug with a knife could know for sure that help would come quickly. It inspired both admiration and gratitude to see six large men in black and white-chequered caps move in a coordinated swoop to seize such a nasty bit of work and carry him out of the department in ten seconds. The remainder of the scene, in the ten minutes before the black van arrived, took place in the confines of the police box.

Encounters with Mr Buzz Fuzz

The violent nature of accidental injury combined with the violent nature of many of those presenting themselves at A & E meant that the young casualty doctors often found themselves called to court to give evidence. This introduction to the processes of the law and to the mental processes of the legal mind was quite startling. On my first appearance, I found myself, without warning or reason, being treated as a hostile witness.

About six weeks previously, I had been about to sign off after the night shift, when six dead or moribund men were brought into A & E from a common lodging house. It appeared that they were the victims of coal gas poisoning. As there were only three casualty officers available at that time, they concentrated on the men who still showed signs of life. It seemed a simple favour to examine one of the bodies. He exhibited the usual cherry red lips of carbon monoxide poisoning and was very, very dead.

I satisfied myself that this was so and filled in a blue card for the unknown man, signed it and went my way. Now here was an angry Assistant Procurator Fiscal asking me, six weeks later, for the name of the patient that I had examined. My explanation about the change-over of shifts was rudely cut short and I was quite unnecessarily reminded that I was giving evidence on oath.

A blue card was pushed at me by Mr Buzz Fuzz, an Assistant Procurator: "What does this say?" he demanded.

"I can't read it," said I.

Mr Assistant Procurator Buzz Fuzz hit the roof and the Sheriff himself took over, demanding to see the offending blue card. He looked truly menacing as he growled: "This is incompetence hiding behind illegibility!"

The whole court looked expectantly at me, a villain if ever there was one. They awaited my reply: "It's not my writing and I still can't read it. Furthermore, this card is unsigned. I think that if the Assistant Procurator shuffles the five blue cards before him, he will find one signed by J. A. T. Duncan. I'm sure that I can read that one."

The threatening atmosphere in court immediately cleared and my evidence was duly accepted. A court policeman caught me at the door of the Sheriff Court.

"This is your first time here, isn't it Doc? I'll show you where to get your expenses."

I hadn't a clue that such things existed, so I followed him up several flights of stairs to the top floor and collected the princely sum of thirty shillings. This money I promptly took across the road to Baumeister's book and record shop, where I bought a recording of Kodaly's *Háry János* suite and another of Aaron Copeland's *Appalachian Spring*. I still have them fifty years later.

Another appearance in the Sheriff Court was aborted by the defence lawyer who had called me. He was representing several miners who had wrecked a social club one Saturday night in the course of a disagreement. Quite against etiquette, the lawyer ran through my evidence in the privacy of a small waiting room. In the end, he said: "This won't help my clients. Sorry, doc, but I'm not calling you. I simply cannot offer you any better fee than fifty shillings."

"That will do very nicely," I said and took it off to Baumeister's bookshop.

There were other very dull appearances in Court, and some curious blank entries in the log kept by the overnight A & E casualty officer. These blanks related to people brought in dead and, therefore, sent straight on to the police mortuary. They included the son of a well-known politician; the wife of another who had been involved in some scandal in London; and a minor aristocrat. In all these cases the police detectives (they were always 'plain clothes') summoned the casualty officer outside to a waiting police ambulance to pronounce the person on the stretcher dead.

It was rather a brusque affair at which the detective would make it quite clear that the young doctor's role was simply to certify that the body was dead. It had to be conducted in the cramped twilight of the ambulance because had the body been taken inside the hospital, full personal details would have been noted at the reception desk. This daily admissions book was available to the popular press, always scanning around for news of general interest. The blanks, however, were news reserved to the Procurator Fiscal and the casualty officer was warned to keep silent.

These negative aspects were fully offset by the last court case resulting from A & E. This also arose from a drunken fight. It took place in a large brothel, the same one that the 'protectors' had fought to defend. A drunken squaddie had slashed a 'girl' with a broken beer glass for rejecting him.

She duly had entered Casualty in the early hours with a couple of bar towels pressed to a gaping wound on her cheek that ran from ear to tip of the chin. She looked like a crumpled mess.

It was 2:30, and the general surgeons were busy, the orthopaedic surgeons were busy and the plastic surgeons were also busy, but their Senior Registrar advised me over the phone to 'just clean it up and close the skin 'til we can do it tomorrow'.

The 'it' in question didn't want to hang around all night in casualty and rejected a big operation that would have needed a general anaesthetic. She was scared; she was in pain and she was shivering cold, but through it, all shone the courage of a street urchin. It was 3:00 am after all this ringing around. The place was clear of other customers and I still had five hours to go. She looked at me and said with all the ignorance and faith of youth: "You can do it, Doc. You know you can."

There was no way out. A thorough toilet of the wound confirmed that, though it was long and had laid the cheek wide open, nevertheless it was oblique and sagging. The glass shard had spared everything important. The facial nerve, artery and Parotid duct were all intact. I remembered the way Iain McLaren had closed deep wounds in layers and I remembered watching the paediatric surgeons neatly closing facial wounds on children.

Her nasty wound took a lot of local anaesthetic and a long time to repair. The final closure of the skin was done with the finest ophthalmic silk in a running subcuticular suture with a bead at each end. We parted at 5:30 in the morning; she into a taxi and I into the welcome warmth of the duty room and its long couch.

Several weeks later in the Sheriff Court, I was asked to look around the courtroom and see if I could identify the young woman who had been assaulted. There were several good looking young women present but no familiar face. When the victim of the attack was asked to stand up, I could only say that she looked a darned sight better than when I had last seen her. That provoked a good deal of laughter in court, but it was true.

There was no nasty scar. This was both a triumph and a problem because I could not remember which side of her face had been sliced open. The Assistant Procurator, the same Mr Buzz Fuzz who had given me a hard time on my first appearance, guided me to the right answer by placing a thoughtful index finger to the left of his chin (away from the jury).

"Now, Doctor, I know that the number of sutures used is neither a surgical nor a scientific measurement, nevertheless, it will give the jury some impression of the severity of the wound."

"As this wound was closed in five layers, including the skin, I suppose the answer must be about one hundred."

The Procurator turned to the jury and repeated the words 'one hundred'. It made his day. The young soldier went to jail.

Being a casualty officer was not so much an education as an opportunity to practice the many bits of theoretical knowledge contained in the medical degree. Over and above all that, it rubbed my nose into the least pleasant sides of our city and there was no reason to suppose that it was different anywhere else. There were long waits in the waiting room of A & E at the weekend, but no question of keeping anybody lying on a trolley for hours while a bed was found for them.

The only people who lay for hours overnight on a trolley were the drunks waiting for dawn to sober them enough to get on a bus. Nowadays, they blame drug overdoses, the elderly, knife crime or psychiatric illness for overloading A & E. The only thing that has not been blamed is the ridiculous attempt to deliver an ever greater workload with ever reducing resources, fed by ever-smaller finances.

A & E performed a useful, possibly even vital, role in Edinburgh's daily life in providing on the spot help for cuts and injuries great and small. In just being there in the centre of the city, it offered practical help and reassurance for those minor problems that GPs, or opticians or pharmacists or district nurses were unable or unwilling to tackle. Simple things, like a piece of grit in the eye, can cause great misery if they are allowed to persist.

One Swiss banker visiting Edinburgh had a miserable few hours with a bit of grit in his eye that, not one, but two large ophthalmic practices in the city had failed to remove. The last one even told him that there was nothing there; that the pain was residual from a scratch. The banker gave me a ten-pound note for taking a large spicule from beneath his upper eyelid, so great was his relief. He thought I was the bee's knees, and, of course, he was right.

Christmas Eve in A & E

My lasting impression of this vital part of any hospital is a happy one. I was on night duty on Christmas Eve 1965. After one hell of a busy night, right up to 4:00, I was awakened from a few minutes of sleep by a Staff nurse who said: "You had better come and look at this one."

A more sensitive soul might have panicked, might have read between the lines of nursing dialogue. Behind an ordinary situation there lay a serious problem that had alerted the Staff nurse's clinical instinct. It was another lesson in the dangers of ignoring the obvious.

A woman of about thirty, looking pale, dishevelled, and miserable stood shivering in her carpet slippers and nightie. The nurse had wrapped a blanket around the poor woman and rubbed her wet hair with a towel. She said that in her carpet slippers she had walked twelve miles through the winter rain, sleet and ice from Dalkeith.

"My husband's been hammering me," she said. "I've run away in ma baffies."

The husband in question was not present to confirm or deny, but 'hammering' was the vernacular for hitting or punching. A quick general examination suggested no reason to admit her to a hospital bed, but, as the hair towel showed traces of blood, caution indicated that a couple of X-rays might help. Meanwhile, the best treatment seemed to be to wrap the poor shivering woman in warm blankets with a few hot water bottles; that to be followed by a mug of hot tea and a bowl of hot porridge.

The Radiographer came into the Duty room almost as soon as I was asleep.

"You'd better look at this skull X-ray. I took a lateral view as well. She's been hit four times with a hammer. Those are depressed fractures. This is big-time stuff for the Neurosurgeons."

So much for my understanding of the vernacular! Once again my trained powers of observation had failed to spot the obvious. This was definitely a case for admission to the Neurosurgeons (or Nutcrackers, as we juniors called them); in fact, it was attempted murder.

The Unique Beauty of the Nurses' Christmas Carol

It was a miserable Night Duty Doctor who was stopped yet again at the door of the Duty room. It was 6 o'clock on Christmas morning. Casualty Sister took me by the arm, saying: "I want to show you something that you may never see again."

We went out of A & E into the dark lower surgical corridor of the Royal Infirmary. Far away at the other end, there was murmuring and twinkles of light. A few lights turned into a procession of many. The murmur became louder and resolved into a Christmas hymn as two hundred young nurses, each carrying a long white candle, walked in their red capes singing through the still and hushed corridors of the great hospital. It was an experience of beauty and one to treasure. Sister was right; I never saw it again.

Training in Anaesthetics with J. D. Robertson

In the last month or so of A & E I was recruited by Dr J. D. Robertson to be one of two new trainee House Officers in Anaesthetics. How he came to pick on me is a mystery, but the eventual outcome was a career in anaesthetics for me. He is prominent among the many people to whom I am indebted for my career.

James D. Robertson was unusual among anaesthetists in that he had made a major scientific contribution to medicine, for which he was awarded an MD. The ERI Department of Anaesthetics contained a great many highly talented consultants, nearly all trailing clouds of military glory. JDR's war record was not for public display. He had taken over the department from a distinguished older man, Dr John Gilles, who had once been called upon to anaesthetise King George VI.

In 1966, his department was to be found crouching in two small rooms under the Scottish Baronial eaves of the Royal Infirmary, in a small corner of the Nutcrackers' suite of cramped rooms.

We two Junior House Officers started on the same day, and so, presented ourselves at 9:00 at a small door guarding a broad flagstone landing immediately at the top of a stone stair. There were other doors with anonymous numbers and a narrow corridor leading away somewhere. At our timid tap on the door labelled 'Office', a red-faced lady of uncertain age appeared. Her scarlet features were not so much the product of health as of the inhaler she was using to calm an asthmatic spasm. This was Dorothy, the Departmental secretary.

In her white coat and fashionable glasses, she looked the very perfect image of an efficient organiser, but first impressions are not always reliable. Poor Dorothy fought a thankless and unrelenting battle with some forty doctors both junior and senior over the allocation of duties and the monthly rota. It was as difficult a task as weaving a tartan blanket and there was always somebody with a bellyache. This may explain why she was so sharp in asking us our business: JDR had forgotten to mention the new boys to her. Being quick to size up the situation, she hit back by sending us straight into his room.

"Just knock and go in."

Dr Robertson looked both pleased and surprised to see us. There were obviously bigger things than House Officers on his mind. Being much preoccupied, he just let his thoughts bubble over across his desk as though we two new recruits were part of his senior staff.

"You two can be the first to congratulate me on having been awarded the new Chair in Anaesthetics by Edinburgh University. I will be Scotland's first and Britain's second, Professor of Anaesthetics. You don't know enough about the speciality yet, so I'll put things in context for you with a little bit of background history."

He was in an expansive mood and there was obviously no urgency about our deployment to departmental duties. We just let him expand.

Macintosh, Morris and an Academic Disruption

The first-ever Professor of Anaesthetics was Macintosh in Oxford, though he was by no means the best-known anaesthetist. That honour would have gone to Ivor Magill who worked with Mackindo, the World War I facial surgeon, and had devised the straight-bladed laryngoscope. Golf and good luck secured Macintosh's appointment. He was the golfing partner of Morris, the car manufacturer, who later was made Lord Nuffield.

I don't think Morris was a very good golfer, so he relied heavily on his partner MacIntosh, who had played since he was four. It wasn't surprising that Morris consulted his golf partner about a surgical problem; after all, MacIntosh was an anaesthetist at the local Oxford hospital and would know about these things. Morris had an inguinal hernia and wanted a local surgeon to fix it privately; did Mac recommend anyone? It, therefore, came about that Mac anaesthetised his pal and made such a good job of it that Morris became convinced of the injustice of the low esteem in which surgeons held the 'gasmen'.

Morris had become a millionaire at a time when they were very rare in Britain and after being honoured in 1934, started giving his fortune away. He proposed to fund a medical school in Oxford and his proposal received the full attention of the University when he put the figure of a million pounds before them. He made one condition, namely that there should be a Chair of Anaesthetics, to which he required the appointment of his friend Dr Macintosh. The Senate of the university squirmed a bit and then decided to let his generosity override their prejudice.

There is a bronze plaque just inside the front door of the John Radcliffe Hospital in Oxford, which commemorates 'the disruption' of the ceremony at which Nuffield was awarded an honorary PhD. These ceremonial affairs are conducted in the Radcliffe Camera entirely in Latin, not a tongue familiar to the motor trade. They also follow a rigid format: the assembled audience is treated to a laudatory address by a member of the Senate, the new PhD is capped, gowned and given a scroll before being led in silence to a seat.

Morris, however, had things to say, so he stepped forward and spoke to the assembly: "My father and mother were simple, ordinary folk. They would have been proud to be present here today."

Academics rustled their papers impatiently, muttering to each other things such as: "Stupid bugger! Doesn't he know enough about these ceremonies to keep a respectful silence?"

Morris continued: "Before I came here today, I put a cheque for a million pounds in my pocket, but as this ceremony ran its length, I tore it up."

Consternation and alarm in the audience caused fresh mutterings of things such as: "Oh bloody hell, we've upset the old bugger," and "We're too snobbish."

Morris resumed after a pause for effect: "Yes I tore up the first cheque for a million and wrote out another for two million!"

Cheers all around. "To hell with protocol; it's been broken already, so let's just act like normal people," was the general reaction.

J. D. Robertson continued: "So here I am preparing my inaugural address as the second-ever professor of anaesthetics. How do you like my props for this speech?"

Dr, now Professor Robertson pointed to two stout bamboo poles leaning against the wall. They looked as though they might be bean poles from his garden. Would he be talking about growing things?

"These are genuine Amazon Indian blowpipes and these small gourds on my desk contain a resinous paste, rich in curare. They're a present from Burroughs Welcome who make the dt-curare that we use in anaesthesia. My research concerned the precise mode of action of curare and you will hear all about it in my inaugural talk.

"I want you two to do a bit of reading today. There are one or two very short introductions that you will find useful. Your first six weeks will be spent with various consultants who will give you practical instruction, but you will be under observation until you are safe to do practical resuscitation.

"The department is moving downstairs to bigger and better accommodation next month; after all, we have more consultant staff than any other departments in the Royal Infirmary, yet we haven't room here to get together for coffee.

"Before you go, I want to show you something special."

He produced a small brown chart, about the size of a postcard, the sort of thing that the anaesthetists used for recording pulse and blood pressure during an operation.

"That's exactly what it is," said JDR. "It's John Gillies' record of King George VI's operation for lumbar sympathectomy. I found it at the bottom of his desk here. It's not going to the college archives where nobody will ever see it. I want it to stay in the department as a reminder to future young anaesthetists that their speciality retains the Royal support first provided by Queen Victoria, who strongly approved its use in childbirth. Not for her any of this nonsense about bearing your children in pain."

"Dorothy will give you your timetables as you leave. See you at the Wednesday afternoon teaching meeting."

Carrying the Cardiac Arrest Bag and Basic Training

We juniors were blissfully unaware that we had started our apprenticeship at a turning point in the practice of anaesthesia. Methods and machinery were producing changes faster than ever before. It was not at first apparent and nobody seemed to notice, yet. For example, the first use of an intensive positive pressure ventilation unit had occurred in ERI only two years before our arrival. Negative pressure machines, the old 'iron lungs', had been introduced twenty

195

years previously, but the new idea of using positive pressure, of blowing breath into the lungs, as an internal 'splint' for the crushed chest had only recently been accepted.

Suddenly, it seemed that all over the Royal Infirmary, new intensive care units were being formed — the coronary care unit, the renal dialysis unit, the haemophiliac unit, the premature baby unit, but, above all, the pulmonary intensive care unit. For the anaesthetists to have a ward of their own was a departure from standard practice. Even the old 'steam wards' which provided a humid atmosphere for the tracheostomy of children being treated for diphtheria had been run by the physicians of the isolation hospitals. Old attitudes die hard and some surgeons and physicians still persisted in their attitude of condescension to anaesthetists. The change came about slowly but relentlessly, like the tide rising in a harbour.

As the use of ether slipped away into the past, so operating theatres were being constructed to a different specification. The century-old nightmare of working with a highly inflammable, even explosive, anaesthetic had caused generations of hospital architects to become obsessed with anti-static terrazzo flooring and 'no spark' electric switches. Clean air and good ventilation, of course, were enduring problems, so operating theatres were still wracked with the pungent odours of Trilene and strong disinfectant chemicals.

As junior anaesthetists, we were among the very last to be instructed in the uses of ether and chloroform. (It seemed tactful to avoid any mention of adventures involving chloroform and midwifery in Cheshire) For the first year, we were expected to conduct simple general anaesthetics using a handheld black rubber mask, and we certainly learned how quickly but gradually to increase the depth of unconsciousness so that our patient did not start coughing; that would upset the surgeon.

We found our new speciality a little more 'hands on' than had been promised, but I think this suited us both. Anaesthetics is both practical and immediate, requiring rapid responses to the presenting situation. It reminded me of my early days in the pottery factory when a mould maker had used the phrase: 'I think with my hands'.

At the heart of the anaesthetist's task is the care of the unconscious patient's airway; everything else becomes secondary to maintaining the oxygen supply to the brain. This being so, the junior anaesthetists became the new cardiac arrest squad, once we had mastered the use of the Macintosh laryngoscope and could be trusted to stick the red rubber endotracheal tubes into the right place. In that instant, we were experts with a badge and a gun, or whatever instrument we were holding. We could even push aside Senior Registrars if the occasion demanded it because we were in charge at the scene of the arrest. This was our showdown at our own OK Corral.

The notion of dealing with a cardiac arrest by the combined means of closed compression cardiac massage and forcing air into the victim's lungs was still new. The junior anaesthetists felt compelled to run like Olympic athletes to get to the bedside before some ambitious Ward doctor could try to open the patient's chest with a penknife. The popular notion of heroic surgery under primitive conditions had caused many young doctors to try to perform a thoracotomy on a patient in cardiac arrest in an attempt to massage the inert or fibrillating heart with their bare hands. Occasionally their daring had been rewarded, but always there remained the problem of dealing with a nasty contaminated wound.

The French have a splendid, rather an evocative term for the anaesthetist attending a cardiac arrest: le réanimateur. It conveys something meaningful about the restoration of life to a person stricken with a cardiac arrest. As the victim's grey skin and blue lips suddenly flush pink with signs of life returning, those gathered around the bed experience the triumph of winning. Admittedly, this was a small victory, not the conclusion of a successful war, but it was still a victory, a goal against the odds.

The cardiac arrest squad consisted of (a) the junior anaesthetist, and (b) a porter to bring a huge resuscitation trolley from somewhere at least five minutes away.

The juniors found that the crash trolley arrived a lot faster if we put our head around the door of the porters' room afterwards and gave them the result. A word of thanks worked even better than a spoonful of sugar with this particular bit of medicine.

The 'on call' junior anaesthetist carried a small Gladstone bag containing three red rubber endotracheal tubes (sized large, medium and small), an Ambu resuscitation/breathing bag with spring-loaded walls (so that we could squeeze room air into the arrested patient until the oxygen trolley arrived), a length of black rubber tubing complete with one-way spill valve, and a Macintosh laryngoscope. Most important of all, when on call, we were given the emergency 'bleep' to carry.

In our first three months, the juniors had a lot of successful 'reanimations'. We were proud of ourselves and so successive failures in A & E hurt our self-esteem to the point where we became desperate for help. We both thought that there was a fault: either we were doing something wrong or we were failing to do something important. It might have occurred to an experienced anaesthetist, especially one who had the experience of military AMFUs, that there was possibly another bug in the system.

The story has already been told of the switched Oxygen and Nitrous Oxide pipes with its finale in the High Court. If it served any useful purpose, it made us wary of even familiar anaesthetic machines and equipment. This was especially relevant in the ERI of the sixties because every operating theatre held different equipment. On first being appointed, each consultant anaesthetist was allowed to choose a new machine. The resulting puzzling assortment of equipment was excused as being a 'good experience' for the trainees, and perhaps that was so.

Before starting any operation we Juniors would routinely check over our circuits, our cylinders and our drugs. Some anaesthetists would rely on an assistant to load syringes and to check all gas connections. We decided that as we were ultimately responsible for any outcome, we should rely only on ourselves and that even then we should be careful.

As a learned judge once observed, possibly in jest: "The anaesthetist bears a heavy responsibility in taking the unconscious patient to the gates of death so that the surgeon can pull him through."

Professor Robertson duly delivered his inaugural lecture on the mode of action of curare and his audience were impressed by his scientific erudition. His juniors were delighted that they were in the Department of such a distinguished doctor. Curare, which tipped the blowpipe arrows of the naked Amazonian hunters, was a natural plant product of the jungle. It is also a potent drug that immobilises the muscles without damaging them.

This is essential to successful surgery in the abdomen and thorax, but curare was the golden key to long term controlled ventilation of the lungs. No doctor who has once seen the sudden onset of the prolonged and agonising spasms of advanced tetanus will ever forget the feeling of complete helpless inadequacy. It is impossible thereafter to deny the blessed relief of the paralysis following an injection of curare. This, however, is only the first step of many to support the life of such a patient and it pre-supposes the presence of an anaesthetist with a lung ventilator machine to provide intensive care for days on end. It was such a patient who led to the permanent establishment of a lung ventilation unit in Ward 19 of ERI.

Ward 19, the Ventilator ITU

Within a year of we two starting as anaesthetics House Officers, Ward 19 moved from being a bit of a curiosity, only to be used occasionally, to being an essential part of the repertoire of advanced surgery. All the junior anaesthetists, and this meant all doctors except consultants, were regularly rostered for duty in the new ITU. An anaesthetist had to be present all the time, so the overnight duties were split between the carrier of the cardiac arrest bag and the emergency anaesthetist on call for night surgery.

There was a doctors' duty room opposite the ITU, Ward 19, with a tiny bedroom beside it. The convention was that the bag carrier could lie on this bed, but not in it. The inside of the bed was for the exclusive use of the Registrar anaesthetist on call for overnight emergencies.

This arrangement was the occasion of bawdy amusement when one of our female former classmates joined the Department as House officer and bag carrier. She was less than amused when she discovered that it was literally true that she would have to share the bed with a hairy one hundred and eighty pounds male. This was not the sort of young woman who would tolerate being messed about. A lacerating tongue lashing was one of her weapons and she certainly had shown her fellow students that she knew how to use it.

She was on the point of taking the matter to Professor Robertson when the whole truth had to be admitted. It would be untrue to say that she took it like a man, when, in fact, she took it like a very angry, red in the face woman who was silently debating which of her two tormentors she would disembowel first.

The ITU in Ward 19 contained four cubicles, divided by chest-high cupboards so that the staff could talk across the room directly to each other in case of urgent need. The patients, being all on IPPV (intermittent positive pressure ventilation) could not speak and were all heavily sedated as well as being paralysed with curare. Four patients, all desperately ill, required constant care from a large team of staff nurses who quickly became an elite and highly specialised nursing unit. Without their daily care, there would have been little continuity in Ward 19. Only one doctor was there from 9:00 am to 5:00 pm, when another would take over until 11:00 pm before the overnight bed-sharing team took over.

This special unit of Staff nurses were the pit props that kept Ward 19's coal mine running. By speaking to their seemingly unconscious patients, they reminded young doctors that the occupants of the four beds were individuals, not just inert 'cases'. It was the nurses who placed transistor radios beside each bed in the hope of keeping their patients orientated by playing the *BBC News* three times a day. They were ahead of their time in anticipating the study of the psychological trauma resulting from prolonged paralysis and ventilation.

At the same time, they took pride in continuing the great Nightingale tradition of full bodily care. They did daily bed baths, they did the bedpans; they would roll their immobile patients and rub cream into buttocks and back to prevent bedsores. They were simultaneously traditionalists and pioneers. The nurses of Ward 19 were the forerunners of the specialist ITU nurses and provided the beating heart of a really successful trail-blazing unit. For nearly thirty years until the Royal Infirmary moved out to new premises at Petty France, Ward 19 never closed.

A Special Patient

Time becomes quite elastic at night, sometimes compressed by emergencies into flashes, sometimes just slowly oozing toward the muddy light of dawn. Night work imposes its own conventions of formal meal times and informal breaks. By its central function in coordinating the movement of the night-time anaesthetists, Ward 19's small galley became the unofficial night owl coffee bar for junior doctors and senior nurses. It was a surprise, nevertheless, one night to encounter in the galley coffee bar one of the Assistant Matrons who was on duty as Night Sister, in other words as night superintendent of nursing.

Assistant Matron/Night Sister had had one hell of a night, with multiple medical and surgical emergencies. She was responsible for providing adequate nursing care for twelve hundred patients, requiring various levels of expertise. At her disposal were some three hundred nurses, not all fully trained. Nurses had been moved from the normally very quiet speciality wards, such as Skins, Eyes and ENT.

Then she had called in 'Bank' nurses, those reservists on standby who wanted only part-time work or who could only work at night. Night Sister had indeed had quite a night and now at 4:00 am, with the hospital under control, she needed to sit down and tuck her grey curls under her white, nun-like headgear. She needed to talk a little as the tension left the tight stretched night-time, and the clock seemed stuck at 4:00 am.

Searching for something to talk about, I mentioned seeing Professor Robertson's little buff card. Her face suddenly shed its weary lines and she became quite animated: "I was present at that operation on the late King. I was Professor James Learmonth's theatre sister for years. He used to pretend that he had stolen me from Professor Sauerbruch, but the truth is that I ran away from Vienna in 1938."

Sauerbruch was the most famous surgeon in the pre-war world and he joined the Nazi party to keep himself at the top. It didn't matter that I belonged to a Catholic order of nurses, nor that I had been his theatre sister for five years; as my mother was half Jewish, I had to go. Sauerbruch gave me a letter of introduction to Learmonth, whom he had met at some international conference, and so I came here.

"James Learmonth was very kind to me and he was interested to hear from me about some of Sauerbruch's methods, but they had little in common. I was with him all through the war and until he retired, so I was most surprised when one morning in 1949, he came to the theatre and cancelled everything for two weeks; no operating; no clinics; nothing. Then he said to me that I was to choose twelve theatre nurses for a special surgical task that would require several days away from home.

Further to this, he wanted me to pack all the equipment and instruments in our theatre because he was proposing to operate in a place that had no suitable equipment, not even an operating table. Everything, he said had to be ready for loading onto a special train at 10:30 pm that very night. We were all to meet in the sleeper waiting room at Waverley Station at 10:00 pm.

"It was some job getting all our stuff packed into really big wicker hampers, but by four in the afternoon it had all been loaded onto these new railway lorries. The table was the worst thing; it was so heavy and had to be stripped down very carefully by the regular theatre orderly. I said to the Prof that this man would definitely be needed, so he was enlisted. At 4:00, I sent all the theatre staff home to have a bath and a meal.

"I don't know why, but I was sure that the railway would muddle up our equipment. The Prof had said that ours was a special train, so there was every likelihood of an ordinary porter getting confused by a change in routine. Sure enough, there was a mix-up. I got down to Waverley at 9 o'clock and hunted out our bulky hampers. That was the easy part because they were too big to hide and too heavy to handle without lifting equipment.

These hampers each had castor wheels, but it took six sweaty men to manhandle them onto the guard's van of the train to Inverness. They really hated me with my German accent for telling them to offload the beastly stuff immediately. A Station Master in a Bowler hat appeared and took charge of the situation. The Prof had been allotted two luggage vans and two sleeping cars, which were to be hooked onto the back of the Pullman night sleeper to London.

"Not until we were on our way did Professor Learmonth tell us what we were about to do. We were going to Buckingham Palace to operate on King George and he asked us not to talk to anybody about it. The press would love to dramatize this operation, he said, but the King was rigidly opposed to any fuss. The operation itself would be one that we had all done before and the nurses would afterwards divide into shifts to nurse him through the post-operative period.

"We had breakfast at the Great Northern Hotel by Kings Cross Station and then we were all fitted into five taxis. We followed three railway lorries in a procession to the back entrance of the Palace. A large sun lounge with a glass roof had been placed at our disposal, but it was totally unfit for use as an operating theatre. Prof Learmonth and I scouted around for something suitable. There was a swimming pool with changing rooms and showers immediately beside it.

The pool, a large area of tiles was empty of water because of the recent polio epidemic and tiles covered the whole poolside area. It was just right for cleaning up and using as a surgical theatre, so we got to work with scrubbing brushes and mops. It took twelve hours, but at the end of it, we had an operating theatre fit for a king.

"The operation was one we had done many times before. Afterwards, we divided into four shifts of three, taking turns to nurse and care for our patients. Although he had a reputation for being very bad-tempered, the King was as good as gold for us.

"We nurses enjoyed being in London. The day shifts were five hours, so we could go shopping or go to the cinema or just rest. It was lovely. The night shifts were longer, but the dear old King slept like a baby. We nurses took turns to sit with the King and he made us talk to him a lot, after all, we were young and fairly good looking, so perhaps he was pleased to have us to himself.

"On the tenth day, Prof Learmonth removed the skin sutures and declared the wound to be clean, but not yet strong enough to go in a bath, so he prescribed showering for the next four weeks.

On day eleven, Prof Learmonth came into the King's bedroom at 10:00 am when everything was neat and tidy. His Majesty was sitting in an armchair beside the bed when the Prof came in to announce his departure for Edinburgh. The King knighted him in the bedroom there and then.

"We all got some recognition, but my memory of the occasion shines brighter than any medal," said Night Sister.

The bleeper at her side summoned her away and I never again got an opportunity to talk to her. There being no further surgical emergencies waiting for the overnight Registrar anaesthetist, I tottered off to the partitioned bed.

The Obstetric Flying Squad & Other Happy Landings

As soon as the young anaesthetists reached seniority (i.e. Senior House Officer) they became responsible for 'covering' the anaesthetics Registrar in the Simpson Memorial Maternity Pavilion (SMMP). The maternity hospital in its 1930s modern Art Deco splendour stood at the South Western corner of the Edinburgh Royal Infirmary's many acres. It was a separate teaching and working unit, integrated into the greater complex of the ERI. It received patients twenty-four hours a day and consequently, required on the spot twenty-four hours a day anaesthetic cover.

When things go wrong in maternity work, they mostly require an immediate response. The SMMP could provide a Caesarean section within five minutes. Its theatres and staff were always at the ready. The same was not true for cottage hospitals nor, most certainly, for domestic midwifery, sometimes called 'kitchen table' obstetrics.

Medical life has few more stressful experiences than to be faced with some extreme obstetric emergency, such as a retained placenta when miles from adequate resources. I had witnessed some of this in Cheshire as a medical student and it was frightening. The patients suffer badly in such situations.

Despite the stubborn persistence of the natural childbirth obsessives, things do go wrong in domestic deliveries, even those attended by a doctor and two midwives. It was to cope with such out of hospital emergencies that the Obstetric Flying Squad had been formed in the Simpson. Many other places in Britain had similar arrangements which performed with varying degrees of efficiency.

In Cheshire, it had been a sham, lacking the essentials to deal with problems in the rural kitchen. Edinburgh had the real McCoy. Its Flying Squad ambulance carried blood, IV fluids, cylinders of anaesthetic gases, a portable anaesthetic machine, a folding operating table and an electrically warmed baby basket. A team consisted of an Obstetric Registrar, an anaesthetic Registrar and two maternity Staff Nurses. They could cope with very nearly everything.

The SHO anaesthetist fitted into the picture at the point where the resident obstetric anaesthetist was called away on a Flying Squad emergency. This person (there were a few female anaesthetists even then) would have performed enough consultant supervised general anaesthetics for elective caesarean sections to be considered trustworthy cover, but not experienced enough for Flying Squad emergencies. There was a row of dominoes sort of system, supervised by Dorothy, the Departmental secretary, for moving junior anaesthetists around so that all essentials were covered. Whatever happened, the Flying Squad got through, even if it had to make do with a consultant anaesthetist.

It was twenty-five years before the ambulance drivers were converted from motorised porters to 'paramedics', so they were not regarded as team members. This was a pity because many of them were eager to be involved and to advance beyond their humble role. I met some of them at St John Ambulance night classes as they pursued an ambulance badge that would entitle them to an extra tuppence an hour. Many years later, in pursuit of material for an article on ambulances to be printed in a small medical magazine I established a friendly relationship with the chief ambulance officer and his deputy.

During the course of several meetings, the idea was developed of a conversion course to change ambulance drivers into paramedics trained and able to perform life-saving procedures, such as endotracheal intubation and electrical defibrillation. I trained these senior officers to become the first three 'paramedics' in Scotland. At this point, the Medical School took over and produced a diploma training course. But here I'm getting ahead of my story.

The ambulance service in Edinburgh endured years of lowly status, underfunding and poor conditions. Their vehicles were converted bread vans, not at all speedy and all with heavy mileage on their clock. It was intended that they should fill a gap until something better came along. Unfortunately, these venerable bakehouse survivors lasted so well that this gap stretched wider and wider. Until recently, they lacked the excitement and glamour of TV appeal needed to attract the attention of politicians and the public, so they stood low on a long list of NHS priorities.

Given the 'ad hoc' nature of its organisation and the ramshackle condition of the ambulances, the Obstetric Flying Squad performed extraordinarily well in town and country alike. Sometimes, we could be called to the top floor of a tenement in the poorest part of Leith to attend to some poor woman who had collapsed through sudden blood loss, say, following an antepartum haemorrhage (APH). Sometimes, exactly the same emergency would take us to a wealthy house in Morningside. In both cases, a woman would be lying in a pool of blood, pale as death and apparently lifeless.

Only a faint heart sound heard through the stethoscope indicated that life's clock still quietly ticked. The immediate need would be to establish an IV drip and give her some plasma and fluid. This often necessitated a minor operation under 'local', called in the trade a 'cut down'. Just as often there would be no clean towels, no soap and no warm water, so the anaesthetist would rub his hands in 'pHisoHex', an anti-bacterial liquid soap carried in the emergency kit before pulling rubber gloves onto his wet hands and cutting into the patient's ankle to find a vein.

Women such as these, who have lost a lot of blood, do not travel well in shaky, bumpy old vehicles. It was and is far better to restore fluid to their circulation before transporting them. Similarly, nurses and doctors also could be hard hit by motion sickness after and during a ride in the old ambulances, so it was often better for everyone to ask the driver to go slow and easy, especially in the cobbled side streets of Leith. In later years, I returned to the Simpson to gain further experience before entering general practice. More of that later on.

The Anaesthetics Department's Training Scheme

J. D. Robertson ran a splendid practical training rotation for young anaesthetists. For the theoretical side of our training, it was rather lacking in structure. This was directly attributable to the established belief that further degrees and diplomas were the results of individual reading and private effort.

Despite these reservations, the training course for anaesthetists in Edinburgh was a guided ramble through the garden of medicine. To prevent our growing roots in Ward 19 or the Simpson, we were sifted and sorted after a year as SHO.

Those who by then had passed the first part of the Fellowship in Anaesthetics (FFARCS) were expected to proceed to the next stage of training, that of Rotating Registrar. The rotation was as full of tempting specialities as a toy shop at Christmas time.

There was Paediatric surgery, cardiothoracic surgery, Neurosurgery, ENT (ear, nose and throat), Eyes, Dental surgery (very tricky if you haven't been shown how), Urology (plenty of ex-servicemen with gonococcal strictures needing bougies every six weeks) and, to trump the lot, Psychiatric hospitals all over the Lothians, requiring a trained anaesthetist to carry out electroconvulsive therapy (ECT). The latter may sound appalling to modern ears, but when done properly (as by me), it is swift, humane and often helpful. There was a further consideration in relation to visits to country hospitals: mileage money for our small cars. Car ownership was the price we had to pay as Registrars for being 'on call' but at home and we were willing to pay for our home comforts.

Royal Hospital for Sick Children

Life played one of its cruel tricks on me in my first rotation, which was through Royal Hospital for Sick Children (RHSC). Tonsillectomy was a very frequent operation in those days and just as frequently it was done as a 'snatch', using a handheld guillotine. At first sight, this was a truly horrifying operation, but when done by the skilled surgeons of RHSC, it was literally a fifty seconds procedure, though not entirely bloodless. Every fiftieth patient or so would require another anaesthetic to tie off a bleeding tonsillar artery.

For the novice anaesthetist, such an anaesthetic was a baptism of blood and fire. In my third week in RHSC, I was advised that our three-year-old first son needed his tonsils removed. Our family GP had booked him into Sick Kids. I could only pray that he would not have a secondary bleed—and he didn't.

RHSC (Sick Kids) was an elderly red sandstone building in late Victorian style, which meant that it had an imposing frontage and a shabby rear. Popular wit recorded this as: 'Fur coat and nae knickers'. Dysentery was a frequent visitor to the children's wards and inevitably I eventually took it home with me. Ordered to stay at home by the City's Medical Officer of Health, until I had produced three clean stool specimens, the remorseless logic of emergency work decided otherwise.

My consultant colleagues at Sick Kids went along with this order until the weekend when the usual Saturday emergencies threatened to get out of hand. I was ordered to get on my bike and come in right away. As a reward for my dedication, my wallet was stolen out of my jacket, hanging in the theatre changing rooms. This was, after all, an elderly hospital from earlier days before security and sterile areas.

Paediatric surgery was also performed in Leith at a small hospital originally founded and funded by the Leith Docks and Harbour Board. It was adequate, but only just so. It was no surprise, therefore, to discover that the paediatric theatre was to be upgraded in the Autumn. On the date duly fixed for resuming work there, I turned up and was about to put my first patient to sleep, when Theatre Sister entered with a face so heavy with thunder that it should have been reported in the weather forecast. She took the consultant surgeon by the arm, saying: "Come and look at the nurses' changing room."

The toilets had been ripped out and replaced by six tiny little WCs facing a row of tiny washbasins at a height of thirty centimetres. Fearing the inevitable, the surgeon turned to inspect the washing arrangements in the theatre. Paediatric basins at a height of thirty centimetres again challenged his lumbago wracked back. The hospital manager was summoned; indignation was expressed; alterations were agreed.

As a Registrar anaesthetist in Sick Children's hospital, I found myself doing a lot of work with the plastic surgeons. Edinburgh's leading plastic surgeon divided his time between RHSC and a special unit at Bangour hospital. He did no private work and so was indignant to be lampooned in the letters column of *The Scotsman* as a Bentley driving rich cosmetic surgeon, dealing with the vain and wealthy.

He, in turn, wrote to 'The Hootsmon', gently suggesting that, as his car was an elderly Ford and as he had no private practice, a correction might be helpful. A full, grovelling apology was quickly published.

In the sixties, most of the paediatric plastic work consisted of trying to mend the scars of severe scalds or burns. Pulling a kitchen pan from the gas stove or just tumbling into an open coal fire was the most common cause of these nasty injuries. They were nasty because the scar tissue grew quickly and then started to shrink, forming constrictions of ropy red flesh that hampered the full use of a joint. The long term treatment plan was to remove as much scar tissue as possible without creating fresh reactionary scarring. Eventually, after many years of patching, a skin graft might be possible as a final solution for the mature youngster.

The other frequent operation was for the correction of hydrocephalus. A plastic tube was inserted to drain the central ventricle of the brain into the Thoracic duct in the neck. This was a very successful operation and saved many children from an early death. I pointed to my own tracheostomy scar to one of the surgeons after he had performed another 'shunt' operation.

He recognised it immediately as the hallmark of diphtheria: "The last cases of diphtheria that I saw were among German prisoners of war coming into the prison cages of North Africa after the battle of El Alamein. Men coming in with greatly swollen necks had to be separated before they could infect the whole camp. The Africa Corps had had an epidemic of diphtheria and its general, Rommel, was knocked out of action for a year by the cardiotoxic effects of diphtheria."

Working at the Sick Children's hospital was a good general experience as well as being highly specialised, but therein lay the flaw. Highly specialised doctors tend to lose a certain amount of general ability. They become like curators in a great botanic garden; some specialising in orchids; some specialising in roses; some specialising in Alpine plants; some in trees. I wanted my garden of medicine to grow nearly everything from potatoes and tomatoes to roses and wisteria; from well-trimmed hedges to shiny green lawns. I began to suspect that a highly specialised job would quickly become a routine job and then a boring job.

Neurosurgery

Neurosurgery was a high prestige, very academic and a rather condescending, unwelcoming place. Edinburgh neurosurgeons of the 1960s regarded themselves as the intellectuals of medicine and were rather patronising to their more ordinary colleagues. Undoubtedly, they were pioneering surgeons and forceful people who got things done where lesser men quailed. There was an air, however, of 'you others don't know nuffin. You're only the supporting cast in this show'. This was rubbed into me one Sunday lunchtime when I was urgently called away from my roast beef by a neurosurgeon with the startling words: "I've got a patient on the table and he's starting to wake up. I need you now."

This surgeon had obviously felt that immediate intervention was imperative to save the life of the patient. He had decided to operate under local anaesthetic on an unconscious man. He had removed a large slab of the skull to deal with a ruptured artery. In doing so, he had successfully removed the source of pressure on the brain and the man was rapidly returning to consciousness.

In most circumstances, this would have counted as a success. In this instance, however, the operation was only half-finished. The wound still needed to be closed. For the anaesthetist, this was an awkward situation, but not irretrievable. Happily, our patient recovered and was even dismayed that he had no visible scar to impress his workmates.

Although I rotated through Neurosurgery twice and became very familiar with both its acute theatre in the top floor of ERI (the Nutcracker Suite) and its showpiece egg-shaped theatres for elective surgery in the Western General, I would have avoided a career in such a department. Impatient surgeons are par for the course in operating theatres and just have to be accepted, but boredom is, for the anaesthetist, an even more deadly problem. There was a joke about neurosurgeons which is probably still retold: their theatres do not have a clock on the wall, simply a calendar.

Cardiothoracic Surgery

Cardiothoracic surgery was another speciality loaded with brilliant but brittle personalities. The chief, whose name was linked with the first wave of open-heart surgery before the advent of cardiac bypass techniques, ruled this department with a strong arm. His other consultant colleagues, not young men any longer, deferred to him in everything as though he could whisk away their job on a whim. As with neurosurgery, there was a branch outlet for their unique talents, in this case at the City General hospital. The chief did not operate there and the atmosphere there was much more relaxed as a result.

Three associate cardiothoracic surgeons shared the operating at the ERI and through this unique training unit there passed a non-stop stream of foreign graduates in search of special skills. Valve replacement surgery became ever more popular and demanded the use of the closed bypass pump. Two consultant anaesthetists took it in turns to supervise a small team of junior anaesthetists in the running of this complex procedure. With so many juniors around for these long operations, there was always a chance for one or another to slip out to the theatre restroom for a coffee. There was a battery radio there on which we could hear cricket scores and news bulletins.

In June 1967, the news of the Arab Israeli war suddenly burst upon us. Operating that day was in the hands of a Jewish consultant surgeon and he arrived in theatre at 8:00 looking very grim. His assistant was a very pleasant young Egyptian Registrar, who came to the table looking very pleased with life. Throughout that long morning, both men behaved impeccably as the half-hourly news bulletins from the coffee room showed the balance of military advantage swing in Israel's favour. Neither man made any comment as they left the theatre, nor was the matter ever again mentioned between them.

The City General had been used first as a TB isolation hospital, later expanding into a fever hospital breathing the fresh air of the Pentland Hills, perfumed with the scent of a large pine plantation on three sides. True to the Nightingale tradition, most of its corridors were open to the four winds, offering only a slate roof against rain.

As TB had receded from a major problem to an occasional infection, so the various wards and facilities of the General had been turned to other uses. In relieving pressure on the various specialist units in Edinburgh, space had been found for ENT surgery, renal medicine and respiratory medicine, including cardiothoracic surgery.

Open Heart Surgery, Old Style

It had long been known that many Canadian children had survived as long as thirty minutes total immersion under the ice covering the many lakes and ponds. The early cardiac surgeons explored the possibility of hypothermic surgery on the arrested heart.

It was an eye-opener for me to assist as a second anaesthetist as the loquacious surgeon performed open-heart surgery without bypass on children of between three and eight. The success of the operation depended on cooling the child until its heart arrested, at which point the surgeon would have an absolute maximum of ten minutes to repair a patent ductus in an inert heart. At the end of ten minutes, the child's brain would be perilously low in oxygen. This demanded that the circulation be restarted and the blood oxygen level be restored to normal by positive pressure ventilation.

The child would be anaesthetised with chloroform to speedily induce sleep and to produce a profound dilation of the blood vessels. The technique depended on diverting as much as possible of the circulating blood to the skin surface, where it could be cooled. Chloroform is a very potent agent in this and all other respects. The consultant anaesthetist, Dr Griffiths (the MO from Kohima) was one of the few remaining maestros of the chloroform era and probably the only consultant in Edinburgh familiar with the findings of the 1938 Hyderabad Commission report on its use. This was not surprising, as he had been a medical student in Calcutta at the time. In later years Indian post-graduates were delighted to shake hands with a Calcutta graduate holding such an important position as anaesthetist to the Regis Professor of Surgery (late Brigadier Surgeon XIV Army in Burma).

The next stages of this horrifyingly intense display of skill and sheer virtuosity vividly illustrated the quote about the anaesthetist taking patients to the very gates of death so that the surgeon could pull them through. This was no joke and this work was performed under conditions of great stress. The atmosphere was icily brittle. Silence gripped the entire theatre, while the big clock measured out the patient's endurance.

The child was given a huge dose of tubocurarine to allow the insertion of an endotracheal tube and to intensify the vasodilation. As a red flush spread over the whole body, the unconscious intubated child was lowered into an ice bath, and its body core temperature was constantly monitored. At about twenty-seven degrees Fahrenheit, the heart grew slower and feebler until it stopped between twenty-seven and twenty-four degrees. A large clock began noisily to record the seconds as the little body was lifted out of the ice bath and placed onto the operating table. The surgeon reckoned to take eight minutes to perform the heart surgery (but sometimes took ten).

At ten minutes, the circulation of oxygenated blood would have to be restored to the brain. It was a matter of amazement to watch the intensely concentrated surgeon as he raced the clock through an operation that he knew very well. When the heart was closed, the rest of the operation could proceed more slowly as warm towels were applied to the child's body and core body temperature was restored to normal. It was generally not possible to restart the heart at temperatures lower than thirty-two degrees Fahrenheit, but as the core temperature passed 32F, small paddle electrodes were applied to the heart to stimulate it to beat again.

These children always had to be nursed with assisted ventilation for the next twenty-four hours, but they nearly always displayed the remarkable resilience of youth. It still amazes me that their post-operative pain should so rapidly have been relieved by ice cream and jelly.

The Great Crash Hamper Debacle

The sixties was a time of vigorous new clinical initiatives, but not all were a success and some were even failures. It had been decided that there should be a surgical emergency response unit, like the Maternity Flying Squad. On the spot, help should be available to assist the badly injured, resuscitate shocked casualties and stop major bleeding. It had fitted the expansive mood of the time, but it lacked a coordinator to exercise and organise this informal, ill identified team. Over later years, the concept was developed and eventually, not only ran out of funding but out of usefulness.

The Surgical Flying Team started with a giant wicker white elephant of a laundry hamper. This prototype for the Surgical Flying Squad was installed in a special locked room in A & E. It contained drugs and instruments to be used at the scene of an accident. It had so happened that a month or two after the installation of this resuscitation hamper into its locked room, there occurred an awful accident requiring, so it was thought, immediate surgical help.

A couple of young men had decided to earn a shilling or two by cleaning windows in the tenements of the St Leonards district, not one of the richest areas. They tackled their task with the old sash windows by stepping out onto the broad stone window ledges. Ladders for this task were out of the question and most housewives would clean the sash outside in two approaches. The top half of the sash would be lowered and the housewife would lean out and clean the windows of the top with a sponge or cloth.

Traditionally, the lower half of the sash could be swung inward for cleaning, but if this was a fixed slide, then it would be necessary to sit on the window ledge, wedge the top sash and wash the outside glass of the lower part. Quite a performance! Our two novice window cleaners decided that a bit of 'derring do' could shorten this and earn them a lot of money.

Unfortunately, so the story went, they had spent some of their earnings on beer at midday. One of them subsequently slipped from the third floor of a tenement and was impaled vertically on the iron spikes protecting the basement area. The horrified police discovered that he was still very much alive when they arrived just five minutes later. He was, skewered by three widely spaced iron spikes running vertically up his body and he showed no immediate signs of dying.

The ambulance crew could not extract him from his barbaric impalement. There was no question of just seizing the man by his ears and pulling hard; a surgeon would seem to be required to cut him out. The call went out for the new Surgical Flying Squad.

The scene at A & E was one of complete chaos. The ambulance men said immediately that the crash hamper could not be fitted into their vans, which were far too narrow. The fire brigade was called to carry the big basket to the scene of the accident. Nobody knew where to find the key to the small locked room, so the leading fireman just smashed the padlocks off with his hand axe. That was only the start. The special door had been fitted after the insertion of the basket into the small room, which had probably been designed to house a WC.

Again the fireman wielded his axe and took out the entire door frame. The giant hamper was wheeled out to the turntable ladder machine. Its ladder was used as a crane to hoist this ungainly load onto the engine and the whole lot sped off, followed by an ambulance full of nurses and excited young surgeons; an anaesthetist went, too. This was to be the opening spectacular of A & E's new unit.

A lot of time had been wasted with these goings-on and a passing GP had stopped by to do the only useful thing so far. He had given the crucified man an injection of pethidine to relieve his pain, which must have been awful, despite the fact that he could still speak with the police. The PCs just wondered, the way they do, whether this was truly an accident. They found it fishy that two unlicensed window cleaners should be slopping around in their good winter coats. This was something that they would leave for later. The scene was now set for the big showdown with street surgery replacing street theatre for entertainment.

The turntable ladder arrived with the hamper and blocked one end of the street. Two ambulances blocked the other end and from them tumbled an assortment of surgical and nursing staff. It resembled the arrival of the clowns in the circus ring. The wicker hamper was lowered to the ground and again the fireman's axe removed the two padlocks securing it.

But the question now arose: What were these anonymous green parcels inside? There was a list of contents, but no indication of where they had been stowed. Parcels were unwrapped and green sterile cloths piled up but the confusion was all too evident. Weeping nurses, pale and angry young surgeons could not even produce an intravenous drip. The GP found a bottle of saline and drip set from his midwifery bag.

Again, the fireman took over. His crew strapped the wounded man to a short ladder. They used their oxyacetylene flame to cut the metal work around him. Secure and immobile, they hoisted him on their ladder.

The firemen had had enough of people who could not do their job properly; they took the man right to the door of A & E on their turntable ladder. It was incredible at the time that the man was still alive, but later it was totally unbelievable that no vital organ nor any major blood vessel had been damaged. The amateur window cleaner ended up in Ward 19 for a week after his operation, while his three five-feet-long spikes formed a souvenir display on the wall of the duty room of the surgeons who extracted them. As for the Surgical Flying Squad, no more was heard of it for ten years.

Yet Another Tragedy due to Lack of Honesty

Ward 19 continued to stitch its way intermittently through my four years of anaesthetic training and, in the end, still had one more major lesson for me. On a grey winter morning, I was acting as the duty anaesthetist in the IPPV unit. Having done the ward round, examining all the four patients and done the usual physiotherapy, a call came through from Blood Transfusion. BTF had misgivings about one particular unit of blood for Mr X and asked us not to use it.

Unfortunately, that blood had been given an hour previously. This produced no advice from Transfusion, who simply said that we were dealing with a mismatch. There seemed a straightforward solution to this problem. With the agreement of the consultant in charge of 19, but who was busy operating downstairs, the man was given a large shot of anti-histamine and another steroid.

Had the true reason for concern been given, these drugs would not have been used; they were totally unsuitable. The sad truth was that this rogue unit of blood had been donated by somebody carrying Hepatitis B.

With hindsight, it seems obvious that Blood Transfusion should have rung all the alarm bells, but they didn't. Mismatched units of blood can occasionally cause an allergic reaction; sometimes, even fatal anaphylaxis, but usually there is no evident change. This routine non-event had bolstered false confidence in BTF and it passed on to me in Ward 19.

At that time, Hepatitis B was to me and to most junior doctors, just another rare viral illness; one that we might encounter in a laboratory or in an Infectious Diseases unit. Twenty days later, we had to recognise it as a werewolf preying upon the staff and patients of the Edinburgh Royal Infirmary. It was hunting for me and for anyone who had touched the infected blood.

Our patient in Ward 19 who had received the blood with the undisclosed contaminant became even sicker and slowly went into multi-organ failure. He was transferred, lung ventilator and all, to the renal dialysis unit in a last desperate attempt to keep him alive. John Clarke was a Senior Surgical Registrar whom I very much admired, not only for his skill but also for his dedicated humanity. He had been deputed to the job of inserting an arteriovenous shunt in the sick man's wrist for the use of the dialysis unit. He had not avoided this difficult and dangerous extra chore.

We met up again about a week later on a Saturday night. He was the waiting surgeon and I was the night shift anaesthetist. The workload was heavy and we were busy at it from 2200 to 0430. In those days the night emergency team received at 11:30 a huge pot of black coffee with another jug of hot milk. This went together with a large shiny steel dish of ham sandwiches and another of digestive oatmeal biscuits.

The Royal Infirmary's belief was that well-fed young people work better than hungry ones. At midnight we took a short break while we waited for our next patient to come up from A & E. We took a couple more breaks for similar delays, so nobody could be quite sure which mug they had used last time, but they all went into the same steeping water and were swilled for the sake of cleanliness. In this way, we shared the Hepatitis virus evenly among us.

John Clarke looked and sounded well, though he did say that he felt a cold or maybe 'flu might be coming on. He looked forward to having a good long lie in bed as it was Sunday morning already; one of the consultants could do the morning ward round of post-operative patients. I never saw him again.

The young surgeon's wife was unable to rouse him for Sunday lunch and he was taken first to the Royal and then to the Infectious Diseases unit at the City General Hospital. He was isolated in a tent but died late on Tuesday. One of my friends, Dr Chris Smith, who was ID Registrar, earned my lasting admiration by inserting IV drips in John Clarke's arms and legs when other young doctors squealed for help or ran away. Chris also stayed at his post throughout the ensuing short but very frightening series of Hepatitis B cases among the medical and nursing staff. There were further fatalities.

On a bitterly cold morning in February, I stood in my battered old trilby in the driving sleet outside a crematorium chapel, awaiting admission to John Clarke's funeral service. His widow had just been informed by the NHS administration that she did not qualify for a pension, as her husband had not been in NHS service for the required minimum time. His colleagues in Edinburgh gathered a few hundred pounds, but it required action by the Scottish Secretary of State to change the pension arrangements.

A serious man pulled his hat hard down against the battering wind and pellets of ice that tried to push him backwards as he struggled up Morningside Drive. Angry and dejected, it felt like a failure to be walking up this cold, wet street simply to save pennies on bus fares. It was time to admit that my career in anaesthetics had hit a brick. A change in direction was clearly necessary, but it was going to need thought and planning.

With John Clarke's funeral, a golden age began to close. I myself reported to Prof Robertson that I had been in close contact with John Clarke and he immediately prescribed a large shot of Gamma Globulin. At the same interview, I had to give Prof Robertson notice that I was leaving the Department in order to take up a post as Registrar Trainee in General Practice. To my surprise, he thanked me for showing an independent initiative. Too many of his juniors passively looked to him to make a career for them and he could not please them all.

Preparing for General Practice

Family practice was the euphemism for general practice, an important part of medicine, but one to which our teaching hospital mentors condescended. Nevertheless, Edinburgh Medical School had just created a Chair in General Practice and had set about introducing this strange hybrid flower to its fifth-year medical students. The purpose was to produce medical graduates fully trained and prepared for the quite specific problems of family medicine.

GPs were regarded as second class doctors who had fallen off the ladder of hospital promotion. That description fitted me, but in its GP Training scheme, the Department of General Practice was offering me the means whereby to convert from hospital medicine with dignity and as a deliberate act, rather than as a fall.

A General Practice Trainee

"Where's my Mummy?"

Asked Daniel, our very young son, as he and I collected her from the City Hospital Chest Unit on the evening that a consultant finally decided that she should be treated for TB. That decided matters for me. Life was again requiring a change in direction. I remembered the gorilla walking unheeded through the ball game. I had been ignoring a gorilla waving a banner inscribed 'feed the family, stupid'.

My exam performance had been poor and there were at least four better candidates for the next anaesthetics Senior Registrar post in Edinburgh. There was a young family to feed and that could not be done on a Registrar's salary. In Edinburgh, there was the additional cost of private education.

While South Morningside Primary School may have been ideal for 'Maisie' the cat in the children's storybook, later secondary education in Edinburgh was more or less in the hands of the private sector.

The very idea of my two-year-old son undergoing an educational test that would decide the whole course of his education was arrant nonsense. It revealed the stupid snobbery of the Edinburgh middle classes and the price that they were willing to pay to maintain social class divisions. The prospect of paying heavy fees for three boys to receive a grammar school type of education that in England was free forced upon us both the fact that we would have to leave Edinburgh soon.

The obvious solution was General Practice. There was a conversion course readily available to ensure that the new trainee entrant into GP work would land on both feet. It was to be a deliberate leap and not a tumble from the hospital ladder. These days, trainee courses cover three years and conclude with an examination for membership of the College of General Practitioners. My traineeship was over eighteen months and I was advised that the MRCGP, as a lesser qualification, would devalue my Fellowship in anaesthetics and not look good on a CV.

My next job would have to be in obstetrics in the Simpson Maternity Pavilion, that great Art Deco concrete and glass assertion of professional pride claiming its share of the ERI frontage onto the parkland of The Meadows. In those days, doctors regarded women and babies as being at the heart of the family practice, necessitating the possession of the diploma in obstetrics (DRCOGS). It seemed a little unfair that the midwives at the Simpson should receive on qualifying as a state certificated midwife, an enamel badge with a beautiful blue butterfly on it, whereas I could look forward to nothing better than permission to inscribe on a brass nameplate six obscure initials. The blue butterfly harked back to the Burmese butterfly inscribed (at his request) on the gravestone of Sir James Y. Simpson.

The Buddhist belief had appealed to him that, at death, the soul flies out of the body in the form of a large blue butterfly. A student of Victorian times might perhaps find in this a delicate metaphoric rejection of his many Calvinist critics who had insisted that labour and childbirth should be painful; that he, with his bottle of chloroform, was defying God's will. These people never go away. The religious extremists persecuted Galileo and Copernicus, criticised Darwin and as late as 1922, used US law to dismiss teachers who tried to present the case for evolution. Today, their latter-day counterparts are signalling their own virtue in a clamour about breastfeeding, abortion, gay marriage, child adoption and many other things that offend their religious prejudices.

The appointment in the Simpson consisted of 'covering' a series of SHO holiday relief jobs. There were twelve aspiring young obstetricians, each to be relieved for a statutory holiday fortnight, so there was plenty to be done. Twelve by two made twenty-four weeks, leaving two for me. The orderly minds governing the great hospital had worked it all out to the day.

Rotating through three teams into three floors of the Simpson with three distinct sets of routines for almost every aspect of midwifery, the newcomer had to adapt fast at each stage. There was a good 'esprit de corps' in the Simpson, despite being divided into three separate units on three separate floors. The obstetricians united in playing as a big orchestra under the baton of the Professor. He may have hammed it up a bit as the matinee idol in his big white towelling bathrobe (by which he indicated that his office contained his own private shower), but he was most decidedly good at his job.

Senior Registrars of the SMMP crowded into the theatre to watch him perform his signature operation: a Wertheim hysterectomy, technically known as a vaginal hysterectomy. It leaves no abdominal scar and so is favoured by those ladies who still aspire to be photographed wearing a bikini. Anaesthetists see all types of surgery and many kinds of surgeon so they tend to be well-informed critics of operative theatricals. Professor Keller was five stars good.

In the Simpson, delivery rooms and operating theatres served as the common focus of activity, with the 'lying in' rooms immediately alongside. The post-natal wards were in three upper flats, and the mess was at the top. This mess, like the ERI, had its own butler and sitting room, no billiard table or separate TV room, but the Simpson Mess evened things by having its own special occasions cocktail of NHS orange concentrate, gripe water and gin. It's quite pleasant after the third one and I felt the same about the job. There wasn't much sleep, but there was a lot of pride in delivering healthy babies to happy mothers.

The mess was rather dated to the 1930s. It was wood-panelled throughout, rather like an Art Deco gentlemen's club, yet male and female doctors were expected to and managed to share the same bathroom area and showers. The floors were highly polished linoleum, a little boys' delight for sliding and skating. At the weekend, there was always afternoon tea laid out in the Mess sitting room.

The three boys thought that their father worked in the world's greatest place, and their belief was strengthened by the discovery that there was always a generous supply of ice cream in the Mess kitchen refrigerator. Judy was not in good health at that time, so she too was enthusiastic about tea and cakes in the Simpson Mess. There was no problem parking a Mini on the grounds of the ERI, so she could simply swoop in and swoop out with a carload of boys.

Our small family somehow came to the notice of Dr G. D. Matthews, one of the senior obstetricians. One summer day, this kindly consultant concluded his lunchtime unit meeting by asking me what I proposed to do with the afternoon, it being my half-day off. The Royal Highland Show was on at Ingleston, by the airport, so the plan was to take the boys to look at the animals and the big tractors. A family ticket was just affordable on this, the cheap day.

Dr Matthews fired up immediately: "Brilliant idea! Why don't you turn it into a family picnic? Look at all these sandwiches leftover from our meeting. Stick whatever you need into the big paper carrier that the caterers were using."

The afternoon was a great success, as was anything containing food for our rapidly growing greedy boys. G. D. Matthew's fatherly generosity typified for me the warm family atmosphere of this great training hospital. I owe him my warmest thanks (and the price of a packed lunch) for making my day off truly exceptional.

My turn for leave came in June and we went to a fisherman's cottage at St Abb's Head, not far from Edinburgh. With our three little boys, we made a model family on the seaside sands. Toward the end of our stay, I felt unwell and my urine turned dark brown. This was a hundred days or so after John Clarke's funeral and was the average incubation time for Hepatitis B.

The prospect of early death rather dampened my performance at an interview two days later for a job in General Practice in Leith. My indifference to life wore off as quickly as my brief illness wore off and my urine cleared of colour. As so often happens after touching rock bottom, things rapidly improved.

Unexpectedly, Dr A. Cruikshank, a distinguished old-time family doctor at Church Hill in Morningside offered to take me on as a trainee GP. Here, once again, I owe a great debt of gratitude. He was into his seventies already, but due to the sudden and unexpected death of his younger brother, he was postponing retirement.

In those days, the GP could set his own retirement date, so his decision was my good fortune. He possessed a Fellowship in the Edinburgh College of Physicians and had been an honorary consultant in the Royal during the war. His was an opinion to heed. This kindly man was very good at deploying great medical skill, balanced by human warmth and long experience of the foibles and strengths of everyday people.

When I describe him as very much Edinburgh Morningside, beware. He was a shining example of all that was good about Edinburgh medical practice and about the traditional Edinburgh middle class. A gentleman, his practice extended from the tenements behind the Union rubber factory to the titled ladies of the Grange. I have still to see a better-organised practice.

Politicians love to mock the medical profession as being hypocrites whose mouths can be stuffed with gold. My GP mentor was emphatically not one of those.

He told me a story about petrol shortages at the beginning of the War. The Government of the time rationed petrol and required GPs to produce their petrol receipts for the previous five years. This was no bother to him because he and his brother kept their cars in Jones' garage with the understanding that the cars should be kept filled up and ready at all times. There was a monthly bill for the accountant to scrutinise. The trouble for many GPs was that they had overstated their spending but had no garage bills to back them up.

At the beginning of the NHS family doctors who wished to join were refunded the value of their practice on a similar basis of accountants' tax submissions on their declared income. A great deal of ill will resulted from persistently dodging income tax, only to find that it was a bullet in the foot. Again, Dr Cruikshank had returned a truthful statement of income and was well content with his NHS bargain.

The practice at Holy Corner had a lot of 'outside commitments', all in the good doctor's name. He looked after the sickbay at a boarding school and made a weekly visit to the local orphanage. As a father of three little boys, I found it quite heart-breaking to be surrounded by toddlers all begging me to take them home. I went so far as to make an official application to adopt one, preferably a girl, as we seemed unable to get one for ourselves. We were turned down as 'unsuitable' as we might still beget further children (though we thought that we were too old!). Three years later we produced a splendid little girl.

The heart-breaking picture persisted of dozens of beautiful toddlers being denied the comforts of their own parents and their own home. In most cases, these children were abandoned as illegitimate and resulted from ignorance about birth control. The conviction developed and strengthened in me that it is a far greater crime to summon an unwanted new life into the world than to scrape out from the womb a mass of jelly that has scarcely any recognisable form. To me, it seems obvious that, for practical purposes, life begins at birth, not at conception.

In the summer of 1971, the serious father began to look around for a future location in general practice. We drew up a profile of the ideal sort of practice and its location. Top of the list was schooling for our three boys. Edinburgh, with its insistence on private schooling for the children of professional families, was simply unaffordable.

In England, the newly established system of comprehensive schooling seemed to offer a free education based on ability. So we looked at English cities that had a combination of well-performing comprehensives, large health centres and a university where Judith could possibly get a research job. Leicester seemed to fill the bill, especially as there was an inducement allowance to attract new doctors to this under the doctored city, plus another allowance for domiciliary midwifery, plus an additional allowance for practising in an NHS Health Centre.

It would have been great to join the practice at Holy Corner, but it had to be accepted that there were family members with a stronger claim. Edinburgh itself contained several interesting but not financially rewarding offers. Most of these GPs held on to the old style gradualism of working up a practice ladder for five or even ten years. Having sweated over the oars as the galley slave of the NHS for seven years and being fully aware of the cost of feeding a family, this sort of parsimony seemed intolerable.

Not surprisingly, Scottish doctors tended to look for jobs in Scotland, with preference being given in Edinburgh to graduates of that city, and similarly, in Glasgow, Dundee, Aberdeen, the local medical school was preferred. Southern England showed a similar pickiness. The nearer the applicant got to London, the more focused it became with some vacancies in the BMJ advertising that preference would be given to the graduate of a particular hospital (there were at least nine teaching hospitals in London, whose self-importance was inflated by successive Ministers of Health who didn't know how to handle them)

My travels in a Mini led me to interviews in Southampton (dreadful smell of crude oil), Bristol (principal was a bit odd), Exeter (nice guy but location not suitable for working wife), Oxford (car town practice that didn't seem quite right, given that their patients mostly worked in the permanently troubled Morris factory), and St Ives (their youngest partner obviously smelled a rival). At the end of the summer, as my time in Holy Corner drew to a close, I had still to make a decision. Fourteen years in Edinburgh had locked Scotland into my very being. We had to leave, but it would be a wrench. Leicester beckoned and provided a warm welcome, so we went.

Viewed now, nearly fifty years in retrospect, the years in the Royal Infirmary of Edinburgh seem golden. This is not all sentimental nonsense. Admittedly, they were years of hard work and very little money, but it remains, nevertheless, a matter of pride to carry a CV stating that the bearer had served six years in Edinburgh Royal Infirmary.

High morale among medical and nursing staff in teaching hospitals such as the old ERI carried the NHS through its first quarter century. In the sixties, the gap between health needs and what was provided seemed on the point of closing. The NHS was a winning team.

Perhaps that is what made these early years seem golden. Edinburgh Royal Infirmary appeared to be set on a rock, like an Edinburgh castle of health, steadfast against the waves of ills and injuries, able to cope with anything. In the white heat of the Wilson Government's enthusiasm for advancing technology, the future still looked golden.